American Culinary Federation's Guide to
Culinary Competitions
Cooking to Win!

American Culinary Federation
Edward G. Leonard, CMC

American Culinary Federation
since 1929

WILEY

John Wiley & Sons, Inc.

This book is printed on acid-free paper. ∞

Copyright © 2006 by John Wiley & Sons, Inc. All rights reserved

Published by John Wiley & Sons, Inc., Hoboken, New Jersey
Published simultaneously in Canada

For general information on our other products and services or for technical support, please contact our Customer Care Department within the United States at (800) 762-2974, outside the United States at (317) 572-3993 or fax (317) 572-4002.

Wiley also publishes its books in a variety of electronic formats. Some content that appears in print may not be available in electronic books. For more information about Wiley products, visit our web site at www.wiley.com.

Library of Congress Cataloging-in-Publication Data:

Leonard, Edward G.
    The American Culinary Federation's guide to culinary competitions / Edward G. Leonard.
        p. cm.
    Includes index.
    ISBN-13: 978-0-471-72338-7 (paper)
    ISBN-10: 0-471-72338-X (paper)
        1. Cookery—Competitions—United States.   2. Cookery, American.   I. Title: Guide to culinary competitions.   II. American Culinary Federation.   III. Title.
    TX648.L46 2006
    641.5'079'73—dc22

                                                                              2005008657

Printed in the United States of America

10   9   8   7   6   5   4   3   2   1

To the students and apprentices of culinary arts along with all those who have put themselves on the line in the arena of cookery competitions and for those who will be inspired to do so by reading this book.

It is those who endeavor to be part of the process and embrace the profession and the benefits of culinary salons, competitions, and contests that make progress possible and the betterment of our profession a reality.

Contents

14
International Culinary Competitions *183*

Introduction

The idea of writing and publishing a book on the subject of culinary competitions emerged at the American Culinary Federation (ACF) as the result of the realization that there was no source available to which those in the food industry could turn to learn the workings of the culinary competition arena—and its many benefits to participants. Certainly, the ACF publishes its competition manual, which contains guidelines and policies, but nothing exists to help a culinarian prepare to compete. It is no coincidence that this realization occurred in tandem with the growing popularity in the United States and Europe of these competitions, both nationally and worldwide. Chefs in this country, both individuals and in teams, travel to many national and international culinary venues to take part in cookery competitions, to mingle with their professional colleagues, and to improve their skills and expand their knowledge.

This book is for them. It is intended as a reference for all those who cook for a living but who are also interested in competing. It is for those who want to challenge themselves, push themselves to another level, by putting their skills "on the line" for all to see and taste. The ever-increasing demands of our customers, along with the many innovations, new flavor profiles, and their application to food have influenced the competition world. The cold food displays and the hot food entries prepared today in these competitions reflect those trends, as well as the nutritional habits and the progress of all things culinary.

The timing of this book coincides with the growth of our industry, which is seeing food and its preparation become of great interest to even the general public, apparent in the great popularity of cable food channels and cooking shows. In addition to motivating more cooks and chefs to compete, I also hope this book stimulates thought among cooking professionals, to perhaps reexamine the way they approach food, the kitchen, and their clientele. And even if they never participate in a culinary competition, I hope they gain from the insights and experiences shared in this book, and translate them to improve their daily menus and to the art of cooking in general.

CHEF EDWARD G. LEONARD, CMC
American Culinary Federation President
Manager ACF Culinary Team USA 2008

Acknowledgments

There are a number of people and associations I would like to thank. First, the American Culinary Federation, for providing the tools and support for the education of cooks and chefs, through its culinary competitions and certification programs. To the German Chefs Association (VKD) for always meeting the challenges of the International Culinary Olympics (IKA) and ensuring every year it continues to provide a forum for education and an experience like no other in the world of cookery. To the World Association of Cooks Societies (WACS) for its efforts to improve the quality of all international shows; in particular, Peter Knipp, the driving force behind its communication efforts. Thanks, also, to every member of ACF Culinary Team USA since its inception, who have taken the time and made the sacrifice to represent a thing called "American cuisine," and for inspiring others to carry the torch.

Thanks next to the chefs: Thomas Vaccaro, Brad Barnes, Dan Scannell, and Charles Carroll. They have been with me since ACF Culinary Team 2000, and contributed to our success in many ways. To Chef Steve Jilleba, for taking on the task of the culinary committee and youth team. To the Events Management Department at the ACF national office, whose staff work so hard to support and organize culinary competitions for its members and the industry, and who developed the competition manual, which was the foundation of, and impetus behind, this book.

I thank all the ACF judges who give of their time and knowledge to help others and to promote our craft as a special one. Thanks, also, to Ron

Manville, our team photographer for the past seven years, who always keeps smiling. Special thanks to Edwin Brown, for all of his work as ambassador for ACF; to the ACF culinary team; and to all chef competitors. To Chef Fritz Gitschner for use of his culinary blueprints in Chapter 8.

And, finally, thanks to Chef Ferdinand Metz and Chef Fritz Sonnenschmidt, for their inspiration and guidance. My involvement in, commitment to, and success in competitions is in part due to them.

Why Culinary Competitions?

Cooking performed in a competition setting has always raised many questions in the culinary arena. Why do chefs do this? Why prepare such nice displays then throw all the food out when the competition is over? And perhaps most notably, is a "competition style chef" a special skilled professional who *only* competes? The first two questions are difficult to answer briefly; but the answer to the third question is a resounding no! Chefs who can step into the highly charged culinary competition arena with all eyes upon them and perform at their best in unfamiliar circumstances deserve our commendation. Moreover, chefs who compete perform very well in their own kitchens, bringing much to the table in the form of new concepts and ideas.

 ## THE GROWTH OF CULINARY COMPETITIONS

Venues for culinary cooking competitions today are as diverse as the food prepared in them and the chefs who prepare these foods. Spanning the globe, you'll find these events held in the United States, New Zealand, Norway, Egypt, Russia, Germany, Switzerland, and France, to name a few. On these stages chefs and cooks of all skill levels and in all culinary disciplines perform the great art of cooking, for all to see. These competitions also give chefs the opportunity to take leave from their own kitchens, enabling them to extend their professional network; they provide a meeting place for the exchange of ideas and new techniques, and give competitors the chance to renew old and make new friendships.

Culinary competitions have received greater exposure in recent times, due to television. Cooking channels, popular among the public viewing audience, have created a new and exciting appreciation for and interest in food. In addition to shows that teach cooking methods, baking, and a plethora of ethnic cuisines, these channels also are starting to take a peek behind the previously hidden walls of cooking competitions. People from all walks of life can watch these professionals "strut their stuff" in an area that, until recently, was open only to chefs. In the past two years, for example, the Food Channel on cable television has telecast many of these great events, an indication that public interest in these competitions is growing. A sampling of those that have been televised include:

- The pastry competition at Beaver Creek, Michigan (now held in Las Vegas, Nevada), sponsored by *Pastry Arts* magazine and other pastry companies. This one carries a grand prize of $16,000 for the winning team of three pastry chefs.
- Bocuse d'Or in Lyon, France, which features chefs from more than 20 countries competing as individuals representing their country and its cuisine.
- The Culinary Classic held in Chicago, Illinois, every three years, which features 12 to 15 teams of chefs from various countries who cook for the culinary classic cup.
- *Iron Chef*, a competition-style show in a "kitchen stadium" that takes place in Japan (and more recently in America) and asks a visiting challenger chef to compete against another chef who is a master of cuisine from a particular region of the world. The host of the show has four to six master Japanese chefs who specialize in food from different regions of the world.
- Coupe du Monde pastry competition, held in Lyon, France, which features pastry teams and individuals from all over the world who display the art of pastry.
- The Culinary Team USA hot food tryouts, which are held every three years in different cities. The final tryout is televised from Chicago and covered by the Food Network.

BRIEF HISTORY OF CULINARY COMPETITIONS

The first cooking competition as we understand it was called a "culinary exhibit," where chefs displayed decorated food that entailed much craftsmanship from the garde kitchen. They were designed to display a chef's skill, in particular the artistry involved in the presentation of decorated hams, turkeys, and whole fish. Chefs would decorate with truffle paintings, elaborate borders, colored gelatin, and vegetables cut into intricate shapes. The chef's imagination was his only limit.

These competitions also featured large displays, called grand buffets, produced by the chefs and their culinary "brigades." The hotels and large restaurants also were in competition: they were competing for the right to boast that they employed the "king of culinary art."

But, in fact, there was never just one winner. Many if not most of the entrants would be given an award or other kind of recognition, not only to show appreciation for their hard work but to encourage them to return the next year. For although it was a competition, it also served as a forum in which chefs could interact, learn and exchange ideas, and form links and friendships with their fellow chefs.

At these events, teams of chefs represent many countries, making the competitions a veritable cultural tableau that cannot be experienced anywhere else. One of the largest of these, in existence since the fifties, is the Internationale Kochkunst Ausstellung (IKA), which is held every four years in Erfurt, Germany. It has come to be known in the global culinary community as the "Culinary Olympics."

GOING TO THE CULINARY OLYMPICS
We will review the IKA and other prestigious competitions later in the book.

GOING FOR THE GOLD

Some believe that awards, medals, and recognition are the main reasons why chefs and cooks compete. Certainly it is understandable that talented culinarians would want to take every opportunity to demonstrate their skills and, perchance, to receive accolades from their peers, as well as awards. More important than the awards garnered, however, are a number of less tangible reasons for competing on the culinary circuit. First on the list is education. For entrants, every competition becomes an opportunity to build on their skill set; every practice offers the chance to improve their craftsmanship. Cooks and chefs also enter culinary competitions to improve many aspects of their culinary training. The initial drive to enter a competition may be to compete, but while at a competition, entrants find that not only are they competitors, but also teachers, students, and mentors. At a culinary competition, a chef has the opportunity to:

- Improve or teach new organizational skills.
- Demonstrate creativity in conjunction with sensibility.
- Increase knowledge in culinary techniques, menu development, and new food concepts.
- Learn new presentation ideas, flavor profile concepts, and ways to produce harmony in food products.
- Generate confidence in ability and skills.
- Reinforce craft skills, from knife cuts, knife skills, and cooking procedures to presentation techniques.
- Follow a thought process that leads chefs to reevaluate what they do in everyday kitchen life.
- Facilitate a consistent interpretation of style and philosophy of food.
- Ensure that a chef's vocabulary will include words such as "practicality," "nutrition," "workmanship," "presentation," "creativity," and "concept," all of which apply to everyday cooking and menu planning.

 THE ACF'S ROLE IN CULINARY COMPETITIONS

The American Culinary Federation (ACF) plays a major role in the competition circuit; in fact, many regard it as the founder of the culinary competitions that have motivated this growing trend.

The ACF has a threefold mission for the culinary competitions it approves and organizes:

- To continually raise the standards of culinary excellence and professionalism in the United States.
- To promote camaraderie and educational opportunities among culinary professionals.
- To act as a staging area for research and development of culinary concepts.

The ACF's goals for those culinarians who compete are just as important. They are to:

- Nurture the creativity of individual chefs and cooks by encouraging their participation.
- Provide an overview of styles and techniques.
- Provide an arena in which chefs and cooks can demonstrate the synergy between good food and nutrition.

- Provide a showcase where culinarians can display their craft—the skills, techniques, and style needed to be a successful chef.
- Offer rewards and recognition.
- Generate feedback and insight for the competitors from approved judges, who have the training and experience to do so.
- Provide a way to earn points for ACF certifications as well as continuing education.
- Allow the public and industry to observe the art of the professional chef and cook.

Clearly, the benefits of culinary competitions are numerous. Without them, the culture that is the trademark of the foodservice industry would be diminished. Some of the industry's well-known TV culinary personalities, whom we have come to know from watching them on cooking channels, have competed either prior to or after becoming famous—for example, Emeril Lagasse, restaurateur and Food Network television host, competed when he attended Johnson and Wales University. Leaders of the industry, too, are former competitors, such as Chef Ferdinand Metz, who competed at the International Culinary Olympics (IKA). He later served as president of the Culinary Institute of America and as a team captain and a team manager for the USA team from 1976 until 1988. Many credit him with putting the cuisine of America on the map.

In the chapters to follow, as I address the question posed in this chapter's title—why culinary competitions?—I think you'll come to agree it's because they benefit not only those involved, but the industry as a whole.

Culinary Competitions Today

As stated in Chapter 1, culinary competitions have come a long way from their early days as "exhibits." Competitions today can range from grandiose international events to smaller local community competitions, and include hot food presentations, pastry, and cold food displays, or any combination. As also noted in Chapter 1, the number of culinary competitions is on the rise, offering numerous, widespread, and exciting venues for those who take part in these events. And thanks to the Internet and television exposure, home cooks and consumers, too, are now aware that cooks and chefs from all over the globe compete in food competitions.

Today's competitions may focus on current trends and the practical application of today's cookery. A competition may, say, require the completion of a four-course meal that has nutritional criteria, such as number of calories, grams of fat and carbohydrates, and so on, hence test the competing chefs' knowledge of nutrition. Finding new ways to create good-tasting food that is also healthy is the challenge. For example, as a way to promote healthy eating habits of schoolchildren, the American Culinary Federation set up a competition called the School Lunch Challenge, held at the ACF national conventions in 1992, 1993, and 1994. The competition was sponsored by food companies, and involved many dieticians in the planning of the event. This competition raised awareness that what we are feeding our kids in school is important, and both showed how to improve the health of school-children and teach them to make healthy food choices.

Other competitions may have a very different focus, such as the afore-mentioned Bocuse d'Or competition, held in Lyon, France, whose purpose is to identify the next up-and-coming chefs from around the world, those who are on the cusp of becoming executive chefs and making a name for them-selves in their respective countries.

Still another type of competition is the team event, which requires chefs to work and cook in synergy with other team members. The IKA, the so-called International Culinary Olympics, is among the most prominent of these. Held every four years, the most recent was held in Erfurt, Germany, in October 2004. Competing for medals and top honors were a record 32 national culinary teams from 32 countries, 12 pastry teams, 16 student teams, 12 military teams, and more than 30 regional teams representing 16 countries—plus individual competitors from around the world. Chefs from all over the world take time from their jobs and families to have a chance to step on the world culinary stage and cook at this competition.

The IKA in Germany is only one of many; a few others on the global agenda include the Masters World Cup, held in Basel, Switzerland, every six years; Scot Hot competition, in Glasgow, Scotland, held every two years; the Culinary World Cup, in Luxembourg; and the Culinary Classic held every three years at changing locations in the United States.

On the home front, competitions are held both in major cities and the smallest of towns. The majority of these competitions are sanctioned by the American Culinary Federation and sponsored by companies in the industry to help offset the cost of hosting them. The numerous ACF competitions offer a wide array of categories for today's culinarians; in short, there is something for every type of chef. Many years ago, the categories would require a chef to prepare many platters of food and display pieces that took much time and expense. Now they have been designed to encourage chefs to compete by offering more reasonable requirements and timelines. For exam-ple, a chef in the 1980s competing in category A, the cold buffet category in the ACF venue, was a lot of work for one chef, consisting of the following:

- One cold platter of fish for eight
- One cold platter with meat or poultry for eight
- A platter of hors d'oeuvres with six varieties, eight portions each.

The category was modified in 2001 to require the chef to show more of the modern techniques and cuisine. A "menu of distinction" was included, which comprises a five-course menu made for a special event or themed dinner.

In summary, today, competition focus is on a high standard of quality, rather than quantity. This makes it more feasible for more chefs to enter, and takes into account the time and cost needed to compete.

 ## HOT AND COLD COMPETITIONS

Traditionally, it was at cold food competitions that chefs could demonstrate their traditional training and display the artistry of being a cook. Chefs would prepare elaborate cold displays, glistening with gelatin, and present them on shining silver trays. But these displays were extremely time-consuming to produce, and costly due to their ingredients, so the number of modern chefs entering this type of competition started to decline. Other factors contributing to their declining popularity were new cuisines and the trend toward eating lighter and healthier foods.

SIGNING UP
In Chapter 12 you'll find the current rules and guidelines for both American Culinary Federation (ACF) competitions and the World Association of Cooks Societies (WACS)

Hot food competitions, which were introduced in the early 1980s, first consisted of "Mystery Basket" (also known as "Market Basket') events, so called because the chefs would arrive in the kitchen, receive a basket of food items, and be given a limited time in which to write a menu and cook that menu in front of judges and spectators. Though the rules varied depending on the host, this type of competition quickly became popular among competitors, because the chefs just had to show up with their knife kits and tools in hand. Following the introduction of the Mystery Basket, other hot food categories were launched, such as contemporary competitions at which the chefs would arrive with a two- or three-course menu and have one hour to prepare and cook two portions of it.

Competing in the Cold

In spite of the growing popularity of hot food competitions, the preparation of cold food remains an important skill that can serve to extend a culinarian's overall craft. And, now, thanks in part to the success in the past few years of ACF Culinary Team USA (the team that represents the United States in the international arena), along with changes in the cold food competition requirements (more on that in a moment), we are seeing a resurgence of cold food competitions in this country. Likewise, restaurant chefs are reintroducing and promoting charcuterie items such as terrines of foie gras and sausage, which are made on-premises. These and many other cold food items on many of today's restaurant menus are ensuring that the craft of cold food does not become a lost art. Bringing these flavorful items back to life in competitions and in restaurants is a welcome development.

In the past, cold food competitions focused on presentation. Astonishing centerpieces would be displayed on platters, on which a centerpiece item, such as a whole ham or poached salmon, would be covered in a white sauce and elaborately decorated. To be sure, these items looked spectacular and had great artistic value, but few viewing these "works of art" could distinguish the food on the platters.

In contrast, today's philosophy for displaying cold food is that it should be beautiful as well as recognizable, and easily accessible to diners, while making a strong statement about the chef's craft and his or her dedication to traditional technique and style of service. Last, and most important, it must be pleasing to the eye as well as to the palate and show great taste teamed with a design that is practical for the customer to serve themselves from.

Some Like It Hot

As described in the introduction to this section, the most welcome change—and the most daunting challenge—to the American culinary competition arena was the addition of hot food events. These generated excitement and interest for the chefs, but left many show organizers scrambling to find venues that provided kitchen stations, complete with stoves, counters, and refrigeration.

For the chefs, though, part of the appeal of these new hot food competitions was that they only needed to apply and be accepted to the competition, then show up at the venue and cook. In many cases, even the food would be provided for them upon their admittance to the competition. They did not have to spend hours of precompetition preparatory work necessary for cold food competitions. Typically, in a cold food competition, chefs would spend the night before precisely glazing food items with gelatin to preserve and enhance the look of their entries. They would then set up their platters and, in most cases, work around the clock to ensure they could present the freshest and most dazzling display for the judges. The chefs then had to transport their entries to the venue site, unpack and set them up, where they would be viewed by a panel of judges who would scrutinize every detail. Following the competition, chefs had to reverse the setup process—collect and pack up their plates, platters, and table items. It made for a very long day or two. In contrast, at a hot food competition, chefs enter, cook their hearts out, clean up the kitchen, and wait for the results.

TYPES OF COMPETITIONS

The Mystery Basket

The Mystery Basket competition was, essentially, derived from the ACF's Certified Master Chef (CMC) exam and Team USA tryouts. The competitor receives a basket of ingredients, along with what is called a "common kitchen" of staple ingredients such as stocks, herbs, flours, and dairy items. After reviewing all the items in the basket, the chef has 30 minutes to develop a menu using some of every item contained in the basket. The requirement is three courses: a first plate, a salad, and a main plate. The chef then has four and a half hours to cook and prepare these three courses from start to finish. After the time is up, the "window" is opened. The window is the 20-minute time frame during which the chefs have to plate up all their courses, which are then whisked off and served to the tasting judges.

The Mystery Basket is a true test of a chef's ability to think fast, understand the synergy between food flavors and their profiles, and to work under pressure. Most important, of course, is the chef's ability to produce food that tastes great and looks good.

Contemporary Events

The most popular hot food competitions are the contemporary events. These, for the most part, are one-hour competitions in which the competitor has to fabricate and cook the menu he or she presented, plus five extra minutes for plating. There are many categories for a competitor to choose from, including: chicken, duck, pork loin, game, and rabbit.

In these competitions, the competitor must provide the recipes, all ingredients, and a photograph of their signature, finished dish. No advance prepa-

HOT FOOD JUDGES

Hot food competitions have two types of judge: one tastes the final product, and the other makes sure that entrants follow all rules of the competition (such as not using preprepared items, and obeying sanitation regulations). Both judges' scores are factored into a final score. In some cases, however, depending on the type and size of the competition, a single judge may oversee the kitchen and taste the food.

ration or cooking is allowed. The competitors are allowed only to bring in the whole and raw materials that are listed in their submitted recipes.

In the kitchen, the competitor's goals are to:

- Display organizational skills.
- Work cleanly.
- Follow up-to-date sanitation practices, especially in the area of food safety and the handling of food products.

Needless to say, a chef's or cook's skills are very important. If a competitor sautés, then he or she must sauté properly, following the established procedure exactly. If he or she is making a pastry cream, the liaison between the milk and eggs must be done correctly. Taste, of course, is the most important score: the food must have good flavor and the appropriate consistency, and be cooked to the proper doneness.

Team Competitions

In competitions where teams compete for titles, both a cold and hot kitchen program are the norm, though it is in the hot food arena that competitors take particular pride in showing what they can do, to the public and the judges. In fact, for hot food team competitions, as well as some Mystery Basket competitions, organizers may sell tickets, and guests attending the event will dine on the competitor's food.

Many of these team competitions are held in conjunction with industry trade shows, with a large number of people in attendance. Thus, these competitions benefit both the trade shows as well as the competing chefs: they bring attention to the importance of such events, provide entertainment, and, of course, give everyone the opportunity to enjoy good food.

Specialty Competitions

There are also many unique and specialized competitions for those who excel or wish to advance in one of these disciplines of the kitchen. A sampling of specialty competitions and categories include:

- Nutritional hot food challenges
- Ice-carving competitions
- Pastry mystery baskets
- Edible cold food (As mentioned, traditionally, all cold food competitions were display only. There is now an edible category, but in only a small number of cold competitions is the food tasted.

- Specific team competitions, such as a chef and apprentice competition, a chef with a waiter and pastry chef, and so on
- Student competitions
- Edible works of art, including chocolate work, marzipan, pastillage, and vegetable carvings
- Grand buffet

Another type of culinary competition that has been around for many years is the recipe competition. From the popular Betty Crocker event to the Sutter Homes Build a Better Burger contest, these attract a wide following, as they offer monetary rewards as well as prestige for the home cook and chef. Note, however, that some of these contests do not allow professional chefs or cooks to enter, although many companies that service the professional foodservice industry sponsor these types of contests. The reason is that these companies receive hundreds of ideas and recipes from applicants who are home cooks and chefs, hence they don't have to hire someone to develop new recipes for them.

 ## CONCLUSION

Culinary competitions today are becoming a major force in the industry. It is easy to understand why: these events teach and enforce skills, making all participants better at their craft. At the same time, they make the public aware of new trends in food, presentation concepts, and the talent of all culinarians past and present. More important, they garner for the culinary profession and all its members new respect and appreciation, something all craftspeople need and value.

Philosophy of Culinary Competitions

When cooking is your way of life, you must, as in "real life," form a philosophy to use as your guide; it will cover your skill development, your work ethic, and your long-term goals. Needless to say, a philosophy isn't formed overnight; indeed, it converges slowly, after years of training, working, traveling, and interacting with other chefs and cooks.

As it applies to culinary competitions, your philosophy should comprise the core values behind the planning and creating of food. And to help you with this, you will rely on chefs and cooks who have a culinary competition background. Speaking from experience, in addition to mentors, I found it was important to always have a purpose, a sound reason, for what I was doing. In my case, in every competition category I entered, my goal was to "wow" the judges, so that when they went to the table, they couldn't wait to sample what I had prepared. Serious competitors should also be passionate about what they are doing, and know why they have decided to make competition cooking part of their career path.

Of course, you may need to adjust your philosophy from time to time, to account for changes in the industry and in your own personal development as well, but your basic principles should never change. Yes, the layout of platters will change with current food trends; portion sizes, too, even the type of cuisine, will change, but the fundamentals of cookery and your devotion to the craft should not.

Herman Rusch, the executive chef of the Greenbrier resort in Sulphur Springs, West Virginia, and an advisor for the 1984 ACF National Culinary Team USA, had a motto for competition participants: "Dedication, endurance, and achievement." Those three words are as meaningful today as they were 21 years ago. Anyone undertaking the challenge of competing in a culinary arena anywhere in the world must be dedicated, if he or she is to endure and achieve. Just by competing, participants raise their own level of craftsmanship, and in the process learn to create new food, consider new concepts, and incorporate new ideas. It is just this sort of strong philosophy that nourishes the culture of culinary competitions. Philosophy, in this sense, is more than one's viewpoint or opinion as to how to do something; it involves the concept of sharing with fellow professionals, those who seek to improve their performance in the culinary arena.

 ## WORDS TO COOK BY

Whether I was competing as an individual, leading a regional culinary team, or heading the ACF's Culinary Team USA, staying focused on the food and the philosophy behind it was critical. "Simplicity" and "elegance" were two words I always kept in mind when competing, as taught to me a long time ago by Chef Ferdinand Metz, my mentor in culinary competitions. I recommend you apply those two words whenever you are developing new dishes, platters, and concepts. I also learned that simplicity combined with elegance is the perfect recipe when it came to planning, cooking, and presenting food, both in competitions and in my job and life as a chef.

As all the great chefs will tell you, achieving simplicity, at the same time displaying technical skill, balancing flavors, and achieving harmony and color for the ideal presentation is a daunting challenge indeed—in particular, during competitions. You will face this challenge anew each time you compete. I began competing in 1982, and for the most part, my philosophy for participating in culinary competitions has not changed much during those years: the methods, objectives, and skills remained the same, as did my quest to produce simple yet elegant food.

GUIDELINES FOR COMPETITORS

If you are planning to enter a competition, make a copy of these guidelines and keep them near at hand as you prepare:

- Recognize from the outset that you will have to work hard and devote a great deal of time to the effort.

- Practice and prepare: these are essential to becoming a successful competitor. Simply put, you can't succeed without them.

- Seek advice from those who are both accomplished competitors and from chefs who do not compete.

- Understand the rules and expectations completely (more on this in Chapter 4).

- If possible, do a practice run and invite an approved competition judge.

- Understand the rules and expectations completely. Don't be afraid to be creative, but use sensible combinations of food flavors.

- Believe in your food and the project at hand, whether cooking, preparing pastries, or designing food displays. Understand the synergy of flavors and how different combinations work together to create a flavorful dish.

- Learn the difference between "show food" and "real food," the latter which you cook every day.

- When producing cold food displays that are meant only for show, understand that you are creating food whose flavors need to "jump out"; that is, you are creating the *illusion* of flavors, to make your judges and observers hungry just by looking at them.

- In hot competitions, use fresh food; cook using the proper principles of preparation; and present your food in an appealing manner. It really is that simple.

- If you are a member of a team, understand that the performance of all the players contributes to your final goal. There is no "I" in "team"; it is the talent, effort, commitment, and contribution of everyone that lead to a positive outcome.

- Remember that judges are human, and are subjective no matter how hard they may try to be objective; so if you have any doubt that the judges will not understand your concept or some aspect of it, go with your instincts and produce another idea.

- Never forget that cooking is a craft, and an artisanal one at that. Execute the highest level of skills when competing.

(continues)

GUIDELINES FOR COMPETITORS *(continued)*

- Understand and research the region you are cooking in. If you are cooking and competing in a part of the world that does not serve fish medium-rare, then do not enter a dish that features fish cooked medium-rare.
- When it comes to considering the color of food on your dish, if you focus on flavor, seasonal combinations, and the harmony of ingredients, in most cases, you'll find the color of the dish will be there naturally.
- When laying out cold platters or hot food platters, incorporate strong lines that allow for simple service.
- When entering the Mystery Basket competition, or when submitting recipes to cook, write menus that incorporate what you know how to do best; and use ingredients you feel comfortable with. A competition is not the time to try new things, to experiment with new techniques, or to be overly creative. As a chef you have to decide what might be detrimental and, conversely, what will be complementary to your final dish.
- Commit to the experience—plan to participate in the competition arena for the long term.
- Cold-garnish cold food; hot-garnish hot food.
- Serve hot food hot and cold food cold.
- Be in it for the long-term benefits and professional gains, not for the awards.

 ## COMMIT TO GROWTH

Another part of my philosophy as a chef is to commit to new endeavors and to remain well rounded. How does a chef stay well rounded? You might decide to enter a pastry category of a competition, for example. Undoubtedly, those in the competition who are pastry chefs will outperform you because of their own specialized training, but that is no reason not to enter this category. By entering a pastry competition, you can begin to understand the discipline needed in this area of foodservice—how to use the tools required for pastry, and what the craft entails.

How will learning these different skills—or at least becoming more familiar with them—benefit you as a chef? Consider that you may be offered a job with the title of Executive Chef in an operation that has a pastry department; or perhaps you might be offered a chance to lead a culinary team that has a pastry chef as a member. Your "extracurricular" knowledge of pastry will never go to waste—if for no other reason than to get your creative juices flowing. With an understanding of pastry and its techniques, you may even devise a new way to introduce sweet concepts and techniques into the savory kitchen.

In my own case, I have entered every category in culinary competitions, including cold buffet food, hot food displayed cold, centerpiece work, and pastry, at one time or another (twice I entered two categories at the same time). I have never regretted it.

FOCUS ON LEARNING, NOT WINNING

Another important aspect of your competition philosophy should be to focus on learning, rather than winning, especially the first few times you participate. Gold medals and first-place trophies are wonderful, but the real, long-lasting reward is knowledge. And you only gain that by steadfastly scaling the learning curve and welcoming feedback from the judges and your co-competitors.

Too many cooks and chefs today enter competitions with one objective in mind: to win top honors and gold medals. When this does not happen, they may become discouraged and forget why they originally entered: to gain experience. This is a shame, for they never give themselves time to perfect their craft; they give up on a process that offers so much in skill building and education of cookery. Even those who have been out of culinary school for a long time and who hold top-level positions can learn something new—indeed, competitions can be thought of as continuing education. Chefs and judges, who are more experienced in the competition arena, set the bar higher, and in turn inspire everyone to perform to their highest capabilities. Walking away from the competition arena because a medal has not been acquired the first time out—or even the second, third, or fourth—is to do yourself a professional disservice.

Conversely, should you be so fortunate to achieve immediate success, resist the temptation, after a gold medal or two, to walk away, thinking you've "been there, done that." When your learning process stops, the chance to contribute to your colleagues and the culinary world stops, too.

Sadly, one of the weaknesses of the ACF's Culinary Team USA in recent years has been a high turnover in team members. This is in stark contrast to the 1980, 1984, and 1988 teams, which had the same chefs for three to five culinary "Olympics" (as did the Swiss, the Canadians, and the Germans). Their successes prove that having the same team members raises the probability of success—not just competitively, but in the workplace as well. Those

19

team members have been highly successful in the culinary industry, as restaurant owners, hotel and club chefs, and educators. Many have also assumed leadership positions in organizations such as the American Culinary Federation.

It is experience and camaraderie that result in true teamwork, and makes a team strong. When there is a constant turnover of members, a team must start from scratch at each competition, climbing a costly learning curve. It is no different for individuals. By having as part of your philosophy a commitment to compete, to always do your best, to try to reach new heights, you will not only make yourself a better competitor, you will become a better culinarian in the kitchen every day.

 ## DEFINE YOUR COMPETITION CUISINE

Cuisine can be defined as "a characteristic, manner, or style of preparing food." So when a chef says "my cuisine" or "my philosophy on cuisine," it means his or her belief, manner, and style of preparing the food he or she serves. For example, Italian cuisine is the style and manner of cooking Italian recipes using Italian food products. When a chef plans a five-course menu in an Italian theme for the hot-food-presented-cold category of a competition, it will be easy for judges to define and recognize.

Cuisine can also refer to the style and philosophy of cooking regardless of the food a chef is using. A chef can take that same five-course menu and present it in his or her trademark style. It may even feature some Italian ingredients, or it may have an influence of flavors from more than one country. This, however, would be less easy to define and, thus, not so easy for the judges to recognize—who will then either have to read the menu for clarification or draw their own conclusions.

The point here—and it's an important one—is to have a purpose, to define an objective for your competition entries. Whether cooking classical cuisine, the trademark cuisine of a certain country, or your own contemporary version of a dish, you must have a plan, a vision, as well as the belief that you can make it all come together, so that in the judges' eyes (and mouths!) it makes sense. If, for example, you prepare a cold fish platter with Mediterranean flavor influences and title it "Variety of Seafood Mediterranean Style," the judges will expect, and should be able to detect, these flavors and the theme throughout the platter when judging it. If, on the other hand, you have no defined theme, no defined objectives or flavor profiles for the platter, this will undoubtedly leave the judges to interpret the dish as they wish. This is not a good strategy for success in competition.

CONCLUSION

The purpose of this chapter was to get you thinking about what it takes to participate in competitions. I want to leave you with a few closing thoughts before we move on to the next chapter:

- When you compete, take no shortcuts in preparing your food, even if it is cold food for display. If you do, believe me, you will be found out. (Many judges carry toothpicks or stainless-steel tools to poke in the food; some will even tear it apart to see how it was made.)
- Execute the fundamentals of cooking exactly; don't try to bypass a process or step.
- Respect the food; showcase the main item you're preparing in a way that does it and yourself justice. If you are cooking a loin of venison, make sure the venison is the star; the accoutrements are there to accent and complement the venison, not overpower it.
- Always, always, always, use the freshest ingredients you can find, cook those ingredients as you would for a person eating at your operation, and expose the flavors through the cooking process.
- When it comes to presentation, stick with plain and simple, whether competing in hot food or cold food. Ask yourself: Is this presentation feasible in a day-to-day operation? Create the expectation that the food has been cooked properly, that you know what you are doing. (You'll learn much more about presentation in Chapter 6, which is devoted to the topic.)

Hopefully, I've whetted your appetite to compete, because in the next chapter I explain all about the application process for competitions.

The Application Process

Participating in a competition begins with the decision to enter; then you will obtain an application, organize the information asked for in it, and, finally, fill out the application. Sounds simple enough, but how you go about this process, and the impression you create as a result, will impact whether or not you are chosen to compete. Just as important, the application will serve as the judges' first impression of you, your work ethic, and overall professionalism.

Thus, the decision to enter a competition is not one to take lightly, and the application process is not one to leave until the last minute, nor to approach casually. Here are a number of questions to consider:

- Have you read the application, rules, and guidelines *completely*? Are you sure you understand these rules and regulations? Have you checked whether there are any age restrictions or any other special criteria that you must meet to be eligible? If you're not sure, ask now, not later.
- Have you checked the competition application deadline and competition dates against your calendar? Will your work schedule enable you to

accommodate all these dates—including day(s) you will compete, the awards ceremony, and display removal?

■ If you must travel to the competition site, have you asked in advance what type of facilities will be available to you? You want to verify that you can work and set up comfortably.

■ Can you afford the financial costs of competing? These will include application and entrance fees; transportation and accommodation costs, if traveling to the site; food, table display, china, and tools costs; parking; and others. You may also be liable for late or cancellation fees.

■ Is your sole purpose in entering to potentially win a monetary award? If so, be honest about that, then take into account the costs itemized in the previous point and "do the math." Assuming you win, what will your profit be after paying all the aforementioned costs?

■ Do you have—in advance—the full support of your employer, friends, and family so that you can make this commitment with a clear conscience? Don't forget to tell them about everything involved—the practice sessions, the expense, and the length of time you will be have to be away from work/home.

■ Have you done an honest self-evaluation? Can you compete at the level set by the application guidelines? If, for example, you have no cold food experience, or have not won any gold medals in hot food competitions, trying out for a national culinary team is probably unrealistic. Applications for high-level competitions have very specific requirements that you may not meet.

Keep those questions in mind as you read through the rest of the chapter.

YOU HAVE TO GET IN IT TO WIN IT: FILLING OUT AN APPLICATION PROPERLY

There are some things in life that are not open to interpretation. In the culinary realm, for example, there is only one way to sauté; no other versions are acceptable. Similarly, there is only one way to fill out an application, if you hope to be accepted to participate in the competition: correctly and neatly. The applications says a lot about you, so make sure it looks professional. If you fail to follow instructions correctly, it implies you may be a disorganized competitor, perhaps someone who does not follow directions and execute cooking methods properly. When judges sit in a room and review 50 to 150 applications and recipes, the only thing they have to go on is the impression the cook or chef makes in his or her paperwork. Is the recipe sensible? Did the entrant take care to fill out everything properly and supply all required supporting materials? You'd be surprised at the number of people who fail to do these basics:

- Answer *all* the questions on all forms.
- Fill out *all* the information in the format required.
- Include *all* contact numbers—phone number(s), work and home addresses, e-mail address.
- Proofread their application; then let someone else proofread it for anything they might have missed.

Another reason to be conscientious when filling out your application is to—literally—beat the odds. Some competitions receive so many entries that organizers cannot accept all applicants. Though some may draw the line on a first-come-first-served basis, others make the cut based on the quality of the application packets. Needless to say, those applications that have been incompletely or poorly prepared will hardly rate a second glance. There is no excuse for anyone to submit a poorly prepared application packet. Computers are available to everyone today; handwriting an application is unacceptable, even if your penmanship is admirable. If you do not own a computer, use one at your local library, or ask a friend to use his or hers. If you're "computer-illiterate," enlist the help of someone you know who's qualified to help you (reward this person with a delicious meal); or avail yourself of one of the many computer services firms now available in every community.

With the basics covered, you can move on to the finer points of filing an application. You may want to consider one or more of the following for your package:

- Use high-quality paper that is pleasing to the touch and to the eye. Here, too, the words to the wise are, simple and elegant.
- Use a font (typeface) that is easy to read, yet classy and appropriate.
- Word your menu (depending on the style of competition you are entering) as a means to make your entry sound so appetizing that the person reading it begins to salivate.
- Compile your materials as a professional presentation, one that is well organized and encased in a quality folder or presentation binder.
- If possible, send your package using one of the guaranteed-delivery couriers (FedEx, UPS, etc.) Doing so will not only give you peace of mind, it will guarantee receipt of your package. Chances are it will also earn your package a little more attention by the organizers.

APPLICATION VARIANTS

No two applications for culinary competitions are alike. They will vary depending on whether they are international, local, or regional; large or small; sponsor-driven or chef-driven; and so on. All the more reason to read each one thoroughly *before* you begin the entry procedure.

TIP

When filling in the blank that asks for the title of your dish or platter for cold displays, word it so that you provide all the required information, yet give yourself room for small changes, in case you decide to make minor adjustments during your practice sessions. Say enough, but not too much.

GOING HIGH-TECH

Technology has not left the culinary competition world behind. Indeed, entrants are using high-tech methods to make their applications stand out—for example, programming a CD as a slide show with their food items. And some organizers allow e-mail entries of applications and menus. As a precaution, however, I recommend you always submit a backup hard copy, just in case the reviewer is not computer-savvy or prefers things the old-fashioned way.

Submitting Your Recipe

When you enter any contemporary hot food competition, you will be required to submit your recipes and menu in detail, along with a picture of the finished dish. Your final results in competition will be compared to the information you submitted earlier.

The following are guidelines intended to ensure your success when submitting your recipe:

- Put the recipe in an easy-to-follow/read format.
- List the ingredients in the order of usage.
- Make the steps simple and easy to understand. They should follow the order you will cook the recipe in the kitchen, and make sense to the recipe. If, for example, in a one-hour competition, your recipe calls for an item that needs to marinate for 15 to 30 minutes before cooking, you might want that to be the first step. Or, if you are making a sauce, for which you need to add oil to a pan before you sauté onions, then garlic, then carrots, make sure the ingredients read in the correct order.

HOW IT LOOKS ON PAPER

In many competitions, there will be no cook-off, and not even the sponsor will test the recipes, so the application, the way the recipe reads, and how the picture looks will have a major impact on how your submission is received.

- Follow the procedure in your recipe exactly. If you are sautéing an item, adhere strictly to the sequence of steps required for the procedure.
- Include in the recipe any item that is a "finished product." This is a must. For example, if you will be drizzling a port wine syrup as part of your dish and garniture, you must produce the recipe for the port wine syrup for the competition.
- If you use a classical term, recipe, or technique in your recipe submission, be sure you produce the dish in the classical way; no personal or other interpretations allowed. Consommé Doria is Consommé Doria; leaving out a step or adding a garnish will cost you points in a competition.
- Call everything by its proper name. Using accurate terminology is

ON SECOND THOUGHT

I have seen many chefs show up at a competition with either an entirely new application package or with many changes to the original one, with the intent of handing out the new materials to the judges on-site. It is understandable that between the time you submit your application package and the date of the competition you may have changed your mind about what you want to prepare. But think twice about doing this, as it may not be allowed. Always ask first!

At some competitions, judges hold you to your original recipe and menu. And at others, competition organizers copy original application packages and submit them to the judges in advance. This is done to help judges establish a standard by which to evaluate each entrant. So though you may be allowed to submit a new recipe package when you arrive to cook, doing so may cost you points; or if your score is very close to that of another competitor, that person who adhered to his or her original intent may be favored.

imperative. Do not, for example, call a consommé a soup or a broth, then go through a consommé process when making the soup. The judges will assume you did this as a means to cover up a possible mistake, such as the consommé did not come out clear and grease-free as it should have and so you called it a soup

- If you want to bring in something—say a piece of equipment—and you are not sure it is allowed, call ahead and ask. There is no sense in submitting a recipe that requires sorbet only to find out that ice cream makers are not allowed.

In the appendix you'll find an example application, correctly filled out.

Submitting Pictures of Your Dish

As mentioned above, many contemporary competitions require that you include a picture of your dish in your application packet. Fortunately, thanks to digital technology, this has become much easier to do. Certainly, competition organizers recognize these are culinary events, not photo exhibits, nevertheless, you'd be well advised to provide quality pictures of your food.

You'll find that the cost for a professional picture in most cases is very reasonable; or you may know (or are yourself) an accomplished amateur who can take photos, and perhaps print them as well. If you do self-print, be sure

27

LOOKS COUNT
If the competition you are entering is national or international, or extremely prestigious, you may want to take your application and accompanying materials to a higher level. In a recipe contest that will be judged solely on the recipe and the picture of the completed dish, the quality of the picture understandably will carry a greater weight in the selection process, so spare no expense to get your photos professionally taken.

to use top-quality photo paper, available in all office supply stores today. You can, of course, have the photos developed at a photo store. As for size, go with either 5×7, or 8×10 for even more impact. As for content, focus on the food only; don't include props or other items that detract from the food; and use color wisely. Always remember before submitting pictures or other items with your application packet to confirm that you have adhered to the rules and regulations of the competition (see Figures 4-1 to 4-3).

Submitting Yourself

As noted in the introduction to this chapter, your application is a reflection of you. In addition to the food-related materials, this reflection will come from the personal information you supply.

The best advice is to not get carried away with your "bio": resist the temptation to list everything you've done and everywhere you've worked. Focus on those aspects of your background that are

Figure 4-1
First Plate,
Tasting of
American Crab

Figure 4-2
Main Plate,
Venison

relevant to the competition at hand, and keep your bio short and to the point, drawing attention to your skill as a chef. Here are some "to include" hints:

- List high-level certifications, such as Certified Master Chef or Certified Executive Chef. (This is especially relevant at sponsored competitions.)
- List any previous competitions you've won.
- Point out if you've competed as a member of a culinary team.
- Highlight local properties you've worked at that have a good name or are rated the best at what they do, such as a Ritz Carlton or one of the top 25 private clubs.

This is not to imply that the selection process is "elitist," but hosts do like to have top cooks and chefs in the competition arena, especially when it is sponsored or customer-driven and they intend to publicize the event. So, "if you've got it, flaunt it!"

Figure 4-3
Pastry, Taste of
Autumn

One more thing: many applications will ask for is a personal photo—a head shot. This is common in those competitions that have a limited number of spots available. If you're asked for a head shot, pay a professional to take it. And here, too, simple is best: make sure your uniform is clean and starched; wear a nice chef's hat (none of those cheap paper ones); and go easy on name patches and embroidery. Your final bit of attire should be a "come-get-me-to-cook" smile.

CONCLUSION

I hope I've impressed upon you the fact that the application process requires careful thought in preparation and attention to detail in execution. If you treat a culinary competition application the same way you do the production of food, you should have no problem. Speaking of which, in the next chapter, I talk about that very topic: the preparation of food for competitions.

APPENDIX 4-1   EXAMPLE APPLICATION

Figure 4-4 shows and example application, correctly filled out.

5. SALON CULINAIRE MONDIAL 2005
BASEL/SWITZERLAND

Anmeldeformular für Nationalmannschaften
"Culinary World Masters"
Registration Form for National Teams

➡️ **Nationalmannschaft aus:**
National team from:

Land - Country
....

	Name/Vorname Name/Christian name	Beruf - Position
Team manager: Team leader:	Edward G. Leonard, CMC	Team Leader
Teammitglieder: Team members:		
1. Chef:	Chef Rich Rosendale, CEC	Team Chef member
2. Chef:	Chef Joachim Buchner, CMC	Team Chef member
3. Chef:	Chef Daniel Scannell, CMC	Team Chef member
4. Chef:	Chef Russell Scott, CMC	Team Chef member
Patisserie: Pastry Chef:	Chef Patricia Nash	Team Pastry Chef member

Kontaktadresse / Contact address:

Name/Name: Chef Edward G. Leonard   Vorname/Christian name: Edward Garfield Leonard, Jr.

Strasse Nr./Street no: 99 Biltmore Ave Rye New York 10580 USA

PLZ/Postcode: 10580   Ort/Place: Westchester Country Club

Tel.-Nr./Phone No: 914-798-5270   Fax: 914-798-5271

E-mail: Chefedcmc@aol.com

Datum/date: 22/02/2005   Unterschrift/Signature: *Edward G Leonard, CMC*

Zurücksenden mit Teamfoto an / Please return with the picture from the Team to:
Schweizerischer Kochverband, Adligenswilerstr. 22   **Tel.++41 41 418 22 22**
Postfach 4870, CH-6002 Luzern / Switzerland   **Fax ++41 41 412 03 72**
Email; norbert.schmidiger@kochverband.ch

Figure 4-4
Sample Filled-In Application for the 2005 Culinary Competition in Basel, Switzerland

Anmeldeschluss: 1. Mai 2005 / Deadline: May 1, 2005
5. SALON CULINAIRE MONDIAL 2005
BASEL/SWITZERLAND

National team:

ACF Culinary Team USA 2008

Menüvorschlag

(110 Portionen)

Proposed Menu

(110 Portions)

Vorspeise/Starter:
Trilogy of American Crab, featuring Crab Bisque, Crispy Crab over Warm Spinach Salad and King Crab Terrine

Hauptgang/Main Course:
American Venison Plate with Caramelized Apples and Red Cabbage, Dumpling with Ragout of Rib meat, Parsnip Puree, and Fall Chanterelles with French Beans

Süsspeise/Dessert:
Tasting Plate of Autumn
Vanilla Cream with Baked Pumpkin, Apple Compote, Spice Cake, Cranberry Sauce, Caramel Glaze with Roasted Apple Sorbet

Rezept der Vorspeise / Starter Recipe

Ingredients	Amounts	Yields: 9 gallons
Blue Crabs, live	25 lbs	
Clarified butter	3 lbs	
Onions, minced	2 lbs	
Leeks, minced	2 lbs	
Celery, minced	1.5 lbs	
Garlic clove, minced	30 ea	
Tomato paste	2.5 lbs	
Hungarian paprika	2 oz	
Brandy	1.5 qts	
Blonde roux	9 lbs	
Chicken stock	6 gals	
Fish stock	6 gals	
Sachet	3 ea	
Heavy cream, heated	1.5 gals	
Salt and pepper	as needed	
Worcestershire sauce	3 oz	
Tabasco sauce	3 oz	
Dry sherry	3 cups	
Crab meat blue, cleaned	8 lbs	
Thyme leaves, fresh	1½ cups	

Method:

1. Start the roux.
2. Rinse, split, and clean the crabs thoroughly.
3. Heat the butter in a soup pot over medium-high heat. Add the crabs and cook, stirring occasionally, until they are bright red, about 10 to 12 minutes. Add the onions, celery, and leeks, and cook over medium heat, stirring occasionally, until they are a light brown, 5 to 6 minutes. Add the garlic and continue to cook until the aroma is apparent, about 1 minute.
4. Add the tomato paste and paprika and cook over medium heat, stirring occasionally, for 3 to 4 minutes. Add the brandy and stir well to deglaze the pan. Continue to cook until the brandy is almost completely cooked away.
5. Add the stock. Bring to a boil, and then reduce the heat to establish an even, gentle simmer. Add the roux and simmer for 45 minutes, skimming the surface occasionally.
6. Purée the solids until smooth. Strain the puréed soup through a fine wire-mesh sieve. The soup is ready to finish for service.
7. To finish the soup for service: add the hot cream, then the crabmeat and roe. Bring to a simmer. Taste the soup and adjust seasoning with salt, pepper, Worcestershire sauce and Tabasco sauce. Finish with the sherry, fresh thyme leaves, and profiteroles.

Warm Shallot and Pancetta Dressing for Spinach Salad

Ingredients	Amounts	Yields: 120 servings
Pancetta	5 cups	
Sliced shallots	12 cups	
Minced garlic	6 Tbsp.	
Quality virgin olive oil	9 cups	
Sherry vinegar	3 cups +	
Minced chives	5 Tbsp	
Parsley	5 Tbsp	
Salt and pepper	to taste	
Scallions	2 cups	
Spinach	36 lbs	

Method:

1. Render the bacon and reserve the fat. Sweat the shallots and the garlic in the bacon fat and some of the olive oil.
2. Remove the mixture from the heat and let it cool slightly at room temperature. Once the mixture has cooled, whisk in the remaining ingredients. Adjust the seasoning as needed. Toss the spinach with the dressing for service.

Alaskan King Crab Terrine

Ingredients	Amounts	Yields: 20 terrines
King Crab legs	60 lbs	

For the Mousse

Halibut or leftover Dover sole	8 lbs	
Raw scallops	2 lbs	

Large egg yolks	24 ea
Large egg	3 ea
Unsalted butter, room temperature	14½ oz
Kosher salt, ground white pepper,	to taste
Cayenne	Pinch
Heavy cream, lightly whipped	3 cups
Crab trimmings	2 lbs
Blanched spinach leaves (garnish)	7 cups

Method:

1. Place halibut and scallop meat in food processor bowl and process until smooth.
2. Add egg yolks and whole egg, one at a time, and process after each to combine.
3. Add butter and pulse to incorporate. Season with salt, white pepper, and cayenne.
4. Place mixture in stainless-steel bowl and gently fold in whipped cream, followed by the crab meat. Assemble the terrines.

Salsify

Ingredients	Amounts	Yields: 300 portions
Salsify	30 lbs	
Milk	3 gals	
Water	1½ gals	
Lemons	9 ea	

Method:

1. Peel the salsify and plunge into the milk, water, and lemon solution. Keep the salsify submerged with a thin sheet of cheesecloth.

Blanc

Ingredients	Amounts	Yields: 6 gallons
Water	5 gals	
Flour	10 oz	
Lemons	9 ea	
White onions	3 lbs	
Carrots	1.5 lbs	
Celery	1.5 lbs	
Salt	to taste	
3 Sachets to include per sachet		
Parsley stems	20 ea	
Chives	½ bunch	
Chervil	½ bunch	
Peppercorns	25 cracked	
Bay leaf	5 ea	
Cloves	3 ea	

Method:
1. Assemble the blanc by whisking the flour and water together in order to remove any lumps. Small dice the aromatics and add to the blanc. Also add the lemons, sachet, and the salt to taste.
2. After all the salsify has been peeled and placed into the blanc, place a piece of cheesecloth over the salsify to keep it submerged during cooking. Gently simmer the salsify till just tender, but not falling apart. When the salsify is cooked remove from the cooking liquid and toss in beurre fondue.

Breaded Crab Leg

Ingredients	Amounts	Yields: 300 portions
Crab leg	300 pieces 1 oz	
Flour	6 lbs	
Eggs	60 ea	
Milk	3 cups	
Japanese bread crumbs	12 lbs	
Oil for frying	as needed	

Method:
1. Dry the crab legs. The crab legs should be cut into 1 inch long pieces. Pass the crab legs through the standard breading procedure.
2. Fry the breaded crab legs in hot fat at 350 degrees until golden brown.

Orange Segment

Ingredients	Amounts	Yields: 300 portions
Blood oranges	40 ea	

Method:
1. Section the blood oranges and use for garnish.

Orange Juice Reduction

Ingredients	Amounts	Yields: 5 cups
Blood oranges (juiced)	40 ea	
Orange blossom honey	2 cups	
Good port	3 cups	

Method:
1. Combine all the ingredients in a sauce pot and reduce to syrup consistency.

Foamed Aioli Larger Formula

Ingredients	Amounts	Yields: 3 quarts
Yolks	21 ea	
Whole eggs	3 cups	
Lemons for juice	4 ea	
Sherry vinegar	3 Tbsp	
Kosher salt	12 tsp	
Dijon mustard	12 Tbsp	
Olive oil	3 cups	
Vegetable oil	6 cups	
Tabasco	as needed	

Method:
1. Whisk the eggs lightly. Add all the ingredients except for the oil. After all the ingredients have been mixed, slowly incorporate the remaining oil to create an emulsion.
2. Add the aioli to a charged ISI frothier and shake vigorously before use.

Zubereitung / Preparation
Rezept des Hauptganges / Main Course Recipe

Venison

Ingredients	Amounts	Yields: 125 portions
Loin of venison	about 25 lb/ 7 loins	
Apple-smoked bacon	1 case	
Apple syrup*	2 cups	
Salt and pepper	to taste	
Clarified butter	as needed	
*see additional recipe		

Method:
1. Wrap the venison loins in the apple-smoked bacon and sear in the hot clarified butter.
2. Season and cook to medium rare. Let the meat rest before cutting.

Braised Venison Neck

Ingredients	Amounts	Yields: 120 portions
Bone-in venison neck	12 lbs	
Clarified butter	16 oz	
Onions	2 lbs	
Celery	1 lb	
Carrots	1 lb	
Leeks	½ lb	
Shallots	2 oz	

Mushrooms trimmings	2 oz
Tomato paste	2 oz
Red wine	1 bottle
Port	6 oz
Flour	2 oz
Fortified venison stock	2 gals
Sachet to include:	
Parsley stems	15
Thyme	8 ea
Rosemary	3 ea
Bay leaf	3 ea
Juniper berry	10 ea
Sage	4 ea
Dried mushroom (crushed)	5 ea
Chives	1 bunch
Black peppercorns	20 cracked

Method:

1. Cut the venison neck into sections.
2. In a large heavy-bottom rondeau, heat the clarified butter and sear the neck sections. After the neck has been well browned, remove from the rondeau and set aside. Add into the rondeau the mirepoix and caramelize them as well. About halfway through the browning process of the mirepoix, add the leeks and the mushrooms.
3. Next, stir in the shallots and then the tomato paste. After the tomato paste has cooked out add the red wine little by little. Form a glaze on the surface of the rondeau with the wine and then add the port. Reduce the liquid by half. Singer the reduction with the flour and add the venison neck back to the rondeau.
4. Add the venison stock and the sachet to the rondeau. Cover the liquid with a sheet of parchment and a lid. Bring the braising liquid up to a steady simmer and place in a 350-degree oven for 2 1/2 hours.
5. After the venison is tender, strain the braising liquid and place on the stove in a medium sauce pot. Adjust the seasoning with salt, pepper, aged balsamic vinegar, and some whole butter. The braised venison is now ready for use in the filling.

Potato Dumpling

For the dumpling:

Ingredients	Amounts	Yields: 110 portions
Russet potatoes	24 lbs	
Kosher salt	2 lbs	
Semolina or Cream of Wheat	2 lbs	
Flour	2 lbs	
Potato starch	8 oz	
Salt	4 oz	
Eggs	10	
Egg yolks	20	

Method:

1. Wash the potatoes and place on kosher salt to bake.
2. Remove potato skins and put through a ricer onto a work surface: level it and let cool.
3. Add the semolina, flour, potato starch, 2 oz of salt, eggs, and egg yolks. Mix well.

For the Boiling Water:

Ingredients	Amounts
Potato starch	1 lb
Salt	to taste

Method:

1. This will be needed to thicken the boiling water for the dumplings

Butter Sauce

Ingredients	Amounts	Yields: about 2 quarts
Water or flavored wine reduction	1 cup	
Butter	4 lbs	
Salt and white pepper	to taste	
Lemons for juice	5 ea	
Grain mustard	1 lb	
White truffle oil	8 oz	
Fine-cut chives	8 oz	

Method:

1. Over low heat, stir the butter into the liquid.
2. Season with salt, pepper, and lemon juice.
3. Add the mustard, truffle oil, and chives.

Bread Crumb Topping

Ingredients	Amounts	Yields:
Sweet onion, finely sliced	3 lbs	
Milk	1 qt	
Seasoned flour	2 lbs	
Chefnique chef spice and salt	as needed	
Frying fat	as needed	
White loaf bread (crust removed)	2 ea	
Butter	2 lbs	

Method:

1. Immerse the onion in the milk. Drain off the milk and dust the onions with flour.
2. Fry the onions in hot oil until they are crisp. Drain over a rack and let cool.
3. Crush the onions, and chop the bread in a food processor.
4. Toast the bread in melted butter until golden brown. Mix the bread crumbs and the crushed onions together.

Dumpling Filling

Ingredients	Amounts	Yields: 125 portions
Butter	8 oz	
Onions (small dice)	12 oz	
Celery root (small dice)	5 oz	
Carrot (small dice)	5 oz	
Leek (small dice)	5 oz	
Braised venison neck* (small dice)	4 lbs	
Venison sauce* (braising liquid) hot	2 qts	
Aged balsamic vinegar	2 oz	
Gelatin	2 tsp	
Fresh chopped herbs	1 oz	
Chefnique pate spice	1 Tbsp	
*see additional recipe		

Method:

1. Sauté the onions in the butter until translucent. Next, add the celery, carrot, leeks, and cook until they are slightly tender.
2. Add the venison neck, sauce, and the balsamic vinegar. Dust in the gelatin and stir well.
3. Bring the filling to a boil and let cool in a shallow pan or a flex mold.
4. Fill the dumpling with the cold meat mixture. Lower the boiling salt water to a simmer. Cook dumplings for 15 minutes.
5. Roll in grain mustard butter sauce and top with fried bread crumbs.

Vegetables

Ingredients	Amounts	Yields: 125 portions
Haricot verts, or small green beans	10 lbs	
Salt	to taste	
Vegetable stock	5 qts	
Butter sauce*	1 qt	
Chefnique (taste of Naples)	1 oz	
Chopped fresh herbs	1 oz	

Method:

1. Cook the green beans in vegetable stock.
2. Drain well and season with salt and pepper. Toss in the butter sauce and chopped fresh herbs.

Chanterelles

Ingredients	Amounts	Yields: 125 portions
Peanut oil	8 oz	
Whole butter	8 oz	
Chanterelles	30 lbs	

Shallots	8 oz
Minced garlic	1 oz
Lemon juice	2 ea
Salt and pepper	to taste
Chopped fresh herbs	1 cup
(Marjoram, parsley, and very little rosemary)	

Method:
1. Heat the butter and oil together. Add the shallots, garlic, and mushrooms together.
2. Add the lemon juice, and season with salt and pepper. Finish with the fresh herbs.

Savory Caraway Tuile

Ingredients	Amounts	Yield: 1½ quarts
AP flour	18 oz	
10x sugar	6 oz	
Egg whites	16 ea	

Method:
1. Sift the flour and the sugar together. In a stainless-steel bowl, add the egg whites to the dry ingredients. Mix the ingredients until a smooth batter forms.
2. The batter is now ready to spread on a template. Spread the batter over the template, and bake just until the batter starts to set. Remove from the oven without browning.
3. After the tuiles have rested for about 10 minutes, place back in the oven to brown. Remove from the oven and let rest.
4. Dust the tuiles with the caraway salt before serving.

For the Caraway Salt

Ingredients	Amounts	Yields: 1½ pounds
Kosher salt	16 oz	
Dry caraway	8 oz	

Method:
1. Grind the two above ingredients together until a uniform mixture is achieved, and sift.

Braised Red Cabbage

Ingredients	Amounts	Yields: 100 portions
Onions, sliced ¹/₈"	1 lb	
Apples, peeled and sliced	4 ea	
Bacon, rind removed, small dice	8 oz	
Red cabbage, peeled, cored, and finely shredded	8 lbs	

Red wine	2 cups
Red wine vinegar	2 cups
Sugar	2 cups
Red currant jelly	6 oz.
Salt and black pepper	to taste
Cinnamon stick	3 ea
Cloves, whole	5 ea
Juniper berries	12 ea
Bay leaves	6 ea

Method:

1. Marinate the cabbage as follows one day before it is needed for service: Cut the cabbage into thin wedges. Place into a cryo bag with all ingredients, except the bacon, onions, and apples. Mix well cover and refrigerate overnight.
2. Small-dice the bacon and julienne the onions.
3. In a rondeau, render the bacon until crisp, then add the onions and sweat until soft.
4. Drain the marinated cabbage from the marination liquid and reserve the liquid.
5. Slice the cabbage thin and sauté it in the bacon fat. Add the apples. Add the marination liquid, cover and cook slowly on top of the stove or in a 300-degree oven until tender. Stock or water may need to be added during the cooking process if the mixture becomes dry. Check the seasonings and balance of sweet and tart flavors.

Parsnip Purée

Ingredients	Amounts	Yields: 120 portions
Parsnips	15 lbs	
Heavy cream	1.5 gals	
Kosher salt	6 Tbsp	
White pepper	3 tsp	
Pernod	1 cup	
Unsalted butter	4 Tbsp	

Method:

1. Peel the parsnips and cut in medium-sized dice. Cover them with cream, salt, pepper, and Pernod, in a medium sauce pot. Bring the mixture to a simmer.
2. After the parsnips are tender, strain and place in a vita blender. Purée the parsnips until very smooth. Adjust the consistency with some of the reserved cream.
3. Finish the purée with the whole butter and check the seasoning.

Apple Syrup for Venison

Ingredients	Amounts	Yields: 2 cups
Apple juice	½ gal	
Cinnamon sticks	2 ea	
Bay leaf	2 ea	
Honey	1 cup	

Sugar	1 cup
Vinegar champagne	½ cup
White wine	½ cup
Vanilla bean	optional

Method:

1. Reduce all the ingredients together in a heavy stainless-steel pot until the liquid forms a syrup. Strain and brush on the venison.

Zubereitung / Preparation
Rezept der Süssspeise / Dessert Recipe

Autumn Flavors Pastry Plate

Apple Cider Sorbet

Zeigler's Apple Cider	1 gal
Cinnamon sticks	4 ea
Whole cloves	15 ea
Orange, zest only	1 ea
Dark rum	3 oz
Sugar	8 oz
Corn syrup	4 oz
Sorbet base (from Rose's)	1½ oz
Honey	2 Tbsp

1. Combine, heat, and reduce by 1/3; strain, cool, freeze

Praline Feullitine Crunch
(crunch under the sorbet scoop)

Feullitine crunch
White chocolate (couverture)
Praline paste

1. Use equal parts of white chocolate and praline paste, heat. The amount of white chocolate/praline paste mix will determine the brittleness of the crunch.
2. Toss feullitine with the melted mix, sprinkle on parchment lined sheet pan, place another piece of parchment on top and roll to flatten.
3. Refrigerate to barely set, pull, and cut. Easier to serve from refrigerator (will loose crunch if left in too long).

Hazelnut Cake

Butter	5 lbs
Sugar	5 lbs
Eggs	32 ea
Cake flour	1 lb 14 oz

| Toasted hazelnut flour, cool | 5 lbs |
| Cinnamon | 1½ oz |

Method:

1. Cream butter and sugar; slowly add eggs, scraping down occasionally.
2. Add dry, until incorporated; double-check the bottom of the mixing bowl, because it will not bake correctly if the butter mix isn't thoroughly incorporated.
3. Parchment lined, greased full sheet pan, weigh to 3 lb 8 oz; spread even.
4. Cake freezes beautifully. Bake at 350 degrees for 8 to 9 minutes just until it pulls from sides of pan, light brown edges.

Pumpkin Custard

(actually I used a Crème Brûlée recipe)

Heavy cream	3 qts
Sugar	2 lbs 8 oz
Vanilla beans	3 ea
Yolks	2 lbs 12 oz
Libby's pumpkin purée	3 lbs 8 oz
Pumpkin spice	1¼ oz

Method:

1. Heat cream, sugar, beans.
2. Combine yolks, purée, pumpkin spice.
3. Temper together, bake 310-degree water bath; grease molds if using as an inlay.

Apple Jelly

Gala apples, cooked and puréed	24 ea
Gala apples, diced and cooked	10 ea
Gelatin, gold	22 sheets
Sugar	
Cinnamon	

Method:

1. Cook the apple in apple juice/apple cider. Use some of the extra liquid in the purée. Drain off the excess for the diced apples.
2. Combine the two. Add the softened gelatin leaves. Adjust flavor/sweetness.
3. Spread; will set when refrigerated. If sets, can heat back up to reuse.

Vanilla Bean Mousse

Heavy cream	3 lbs 1 oz
Milk	2 lbs 3 oz
Vanilla bean seeds	4 ea

20-fold extract (vanilla)	4 cups
Sugar	15 oz
Pastry cream powder (instant)	6 oz
Yolks	3 cups
Gelatin gold	24 sheets
Butter	10 oz

Method:

1. Heat milk, vanilla beans, extract. In a bowl combine yolks, sugar, and pastry cream powder. Basically making a pastry cream, slightly thinner.
2. Temper milk mix and yolk mix. Cook; will thicken. Remove from heat.
3. Add butter and softened gelatin sheets. Cool.
4. Whip heavy cream, fairly soft. Be careful: high fat recipe, breaks.
5. Add whipped cream to cooled "pastry cream." Pour into molds.

Caramel Glaze

Sugar	3 lbs 12 oz
Water	3 lbs 8 oz
Cornstarch	3 oz
Gelatin gold	10 sheets
Heavy cream	3 lbs 8 oz

Method:

1. Cook sugar, water, cornstarch, until desired caramel darkness.
2. Add heavy cream.
3. Add softened gelatin leaves.
4. Strain and cool before pouring.
5. If too thick, adjust with water; if too thin, add more gelatin sheets.

Milk Chocolate Cinnamon Ganache

(Thin layer on hazelnut cake b/f spreading the apple jelly)
Cinnamon
Heavy cream
Milk chocolate, Callebaut
Cinnamon Tuile Batter

AP flour	4 oz
Sugar	4 oz
Egg whites	4 oz
Melted butter	4 oz

Method:

1. AP and sugar, add whites, add butter; chill to set up (cinnamon optional).

Practice and Preparation

I t is said that success favors the prepared mind. It's also said that practice makes perfect. When it comes to the culinary competition arena, these are words to live by.

This chapter introduces the three tasks that I regard as critical for anyone to succeed as a culinary competitor:

- Conduct a skills and attributes inventory.
- Formulate an action plan.
- Practice and solicit feedback.

 ## CONDUCTING A SKILLS AND ATTRIBUTES INVENTORY

This task is a self-evaluation of your skills. Because you will conduct it yourself, it is imperative that you be honest. There is no point to this exercise if you are not; you will do a disservice to yourself and your fellow competitors.

The purpose of this inventory is to help you identify precisely your strengths and weaknesses. Your goal is twofold here: First, you want to know all your strengths so that you can make them work for you when you need them most; and, second, you want to recognize your weaknesses so that you can do all you can to minimize the effect they have on your performance. That is, you want to be able to *strategize* so that your weaknesses are never apparent to the judges. By having this information at hand, you will be able to prepare and practice effectively, focusing and relying on your strength skills while at the same time addressing those that need improvement.

TIP

If you have entered prior competitions and took notes (*always* a good idea) on the feedback you received from the judges, review those notes before you fill out the inventory. That feedback will provide valuable—and objective—insight into your strengths and weaknesses evaluation.

To conduct this inventory, I always recommend preparing a skills and attributes list, like the one shown in Figure 5-1. Again, as you take on this task, don't cheat yourself: see yourself as you really are, not as you hope or imagine yourself to be, otherwise you will never become what you hope. This sample inventory includes all the basics you will need to be both a top competitor and a top cook or chef. The results of filling out this list will dictate where you will spend most of your time and effort practicing and preparing for any competition you enter.

After you've completed the inventory, and have spent some time thinking about what it tells you about yourself, it's time to take action.

 ## FORMULATING AN ACTION PLAN

The everyday life of a chef is one of hustle and bustle. It is all too easy to become sidetracked, and before you know it you have missed the deadline for a competition. I have seen this happen to many individual competitors and teams alike. The result is that some do not get the chance to compete because the organizer refuses to accept their application late.

The action plan is intended to prevent that. It will serve as your guide from start to finish for any competition you enter. As such it will ensure that you follow up on items that need following up on and that you make the time to practice and complete all other tasks associated with entering a competition; in short, it will help you to commit to achieving all of your goals and objectives in a timely manner. But—and this is a big but—for it to work, you must review the action plan daily, and adhere to the process laid out in it. Of course, the action plan will have to accommodate your work schedule and personal life, but by following the plan you should be able to meet your competition goals.

NOT JUST
FOR BEGINNERS
Even seasoned competitors should follow an action plan.

Skills and Attributes	Good	Very Good	Excellent	Poor	Needs Work
Menu writing					
Organization					
Planning					
Glazing					
Platter and plate design					
Concept development					
Cooking knowledge					
Understanding of rules					
Charcuterie					
Sautéing					
Braising					
Poaching					
Roasting					
Contemporary food concepts					
Classical cuisine					
Ability to handle pressure					
Ability to give directions					
Butchery					
Filleting					
Garde					
Sanitation					
Ingredient utilization					
Overall craftsmanship					
Serving methods					
Portion-size understanding					
Flavor development					
Textural understanding					
Modern food presentation					
Nutritional consciousness					
Classical cut knowledge					
Classical cut proficiency					
Knife skills overall					
Slicing					
Flavor profiles of other countries					

Figure 5-1
Skills Inventory

Before I show you some sample action plans, I want to give you an overview of the contents of these plans:

- First and foremost, an action plan identifies and charts each action that you need to take from day one after deciding to enter a competition. That means every step of every action, and in a logical order, from sending in the application to the award ceremony. Each action will have an accompanying date of completion that the proposed actions are to be finished.

■ The action plan will also serve as a reminder of small but important to-do items you might otherwise forget while focusing on the big picture—such as making sure your vehicle has a full tank of gas the night before you leave. You don't need the added stress of trying to find a gas station at 3:00 in the morning when you are on the road.

■ The action plan can also serve as a guide for your setup and timing. It's a good idea to time your steps during practice sessions and then record them in an action plan.

FACTOR IN BREAK TIMES

Though I can't stress enough the importance of planning for competitions, I'd be remiss if I didn't point out that this does not mean going to extremes. Don't burn yourself out by over-doing it. It is when we are overtired or under pressure that work becomes unorganized, and we forget a vital step in a classic procedure, or leave out an ingredient. So don't forget to factor in break times to your action plans.

Three Phases of an Action Plan

I have always found it effective to use a three-phase action plan for competitions, as follows:

Phase One: The phase-one action plan can be thought of as the general overview: it lists every action and the date by which it needs to be completed. A sample of a phase-one action plan is shown in Figure 5-2, which uses as parameters an out-of-town competition to be held on March 20, with an application deadline of January 5. (Most shows are announced at least 90 days in advance.)

Phase Two: The phase-two action plan establishes your practice sessions for the competition—so that you get your timing right. Whether it is hot or cold food competition, you must practice and prepare the food to be presented as per the competition requirements. The action plans shown in Figures 5-3 and 5-4 are for a cold food display and a hot food competition (three courses), respectively.

Phase Three: This is the logistics phase plan—getting to the competition site (especially with cold displays) on time, with all food products safe and secure, all tools at the ready, personal attire ready for the big day, and so on.

 PRACTICING AND SOLICITING FEEDBACK

It never ceases to amaze me how many entrants show up for a competition without having practiced or asked for feedback; they don't step through their cold display, or practice-cook their hot food menu repeatedly. Some may still succeed, but their chances of doing so are significantly reduced; moreover,

Deadline for application is January 5; $75 fee

ACTION	DATE TO BE COMPLETED
1. Review application.	November 5
2. Check calendar to ensure time off from work.	November 5
3. Select category.	November 5
4. Cook and practice concepts.	November 5–25
5. Plan category and write menu.	November 30
6. Fill out application.	December 5
7. Call show organizer with any questions.	December 5
8. Double-check application; write check and mail UPS 3-day.	December 6
9. Make hotel reservations.	December 6
10. Rent van or SUV, if needed.	December 6
11. Call show organizer and let them know you are entering and application is on the way. Ask for a return call to confirm the receipt of your entry.	December 7
12. Create action plan with work schedule for practice and departure for the show.	December 10

Figure 5-2
Action Plan for Chefs' Championship, March 20–22

they miss out on the real benefit of these competitions: the chance to learn, to improve their craft. Every time you do a practice session, you learn something new; you find a way to do it better the next time.

Feedback: where would the great cooks and chefs be without it? This is a craft that thrives on interaction with and advice from others. Thus, feedback is a vital component when you are preparing and practicing for a culinary competition. Depending on the situation, you may want to seek feedback from both nonjudges and accomplished chefs. For example, in preparation for one-hour cooking competitions, you may want to prepare your dish first for your manager, your spouse, or some friends. They will give you the very important and valuable customer perspective, before you seek a professional's insights. Another reason this is a good idea is that many good judges evaluate from the perspective of a customer. They ask themselves: Would I enjoy eating this? Would I walk away from this meal thinking it was special?

When you do feel ready to enlist a chef to watch one of your practice sessions, taste your food, or view your platter, make sure it is a chef who either is an accomplished competitor, a judge, or has a stellar reputation as a top

TIP

Do not invite anyone to critique your work too early in the process.

49

ACTION PLAN FOR PRACTICE	DATE
1. Prepare order list for platter items.	December 12
2. Sketch out the platter a few ways.	December 12
3. Sketch each garnish and item, listing all ingredients.	December 12
4. Prepare main item terrine of lobster. Make notes, take pictures, and taste.	December 15
5. Prepare secondary item lobster and salmon roulade with vanilla cream. Make notes, take pictures, and taste.	December 20
6. Prepare lobster and truffle timbale. Make notes, take pictures, and taste.	December 22
7. Prepare and create structured garnish (2). Make notes, take pictures, and taste.	January 3
8. Prepare salad of jicama, citrus, and artichoke. Make notes, take pictures, and taste.	January 5
9. Design and make cracker dough garnish of lobster tail, along with sauces for platter.	January 7
10. Review schedule and allot the time for three full runs with platter.	January 7
11. Prepare mis en place for the whole platter. Record the prep time and amounts needed.	January 9 and 10
12. Start preparation for the platter with all components. Record time from start to finish.	Week of January 15
13. Repeat whole platter production.	Week of January 30
14. Do final run of platter. Invite local judge and chef to give feedback.	Week of February 5
15. Work on glazing techniques.	Week of February 12
16. Adjust platter as per feedback and your own thoughts.	Week of February 26

Action Plan Prior to Competition
Display Date: March 20
Setup time by 8:00 p.m.

ACTION	DATE
1. Start mis en place for platter.	March 13
2. Prepare cracker dough and make crackers.	March 14 and 15
3. Start packing for 3 nights.	March 14 and 15

Figure 5-3
Chefs' Challenge for Cold Food Display, March 20–22

Action Plan for Practice	Date
1. Prepare order list for recipes.	December 12
2. Sketch out the plates for each course. Sketch out the items for each course.	December 12
3. Make a mis en place list for setup. Purchase or secure nice bowls, dishes for mis en place.	December 15
4. Prepare and cook first plate. Make notes, take pictures, and taste.	December 20
5. Prepare and cook salad intermettzo course. Make notes, take pictures, and taste.	December 22
6. Prepare and cook the main plate. Make notes, take pictures, and taste.	January 3
7. Prep and do all mis en place for three courses. Make notes.	January 5
8. Set up station and start cooking all three courses. Make notes, taste food, adjust as needed, take pictures.	January 6
9. Prep and do all mis en place for three courses.	January 7–10
10. Set up station and do a full-run cooking of all three courses.	January 9 and 10
11. Prep and do all mis en place for three courses.	January 7–13
12. Set up station and do a full-run cooking all three courses.	January 14
13. Do the menu three more times inviting chefs to critique and give feedback.	January 18, 22 February 10
14. Session fully timed and competition ready.	February 18
15. Final run 2 more times prior to competition.	March 10 and 16

Figure 5-4
Action Plan for Hot Food Three-Course Chefs' Challenge, March 20–22

culinarian. It is also important to try and find a person who is "in the loop," so to speak, in regard to current trends and food styles. A chef who competed 30 years ago and has not been involved in the competition arena may be able to guide you through a menu calling for classical techniques, but may not be best suited to guide you to compete in today's culinary arena.

One cautionary note in regard to feedback: too many viewpoints and opinions can leave you confused or, worse, repeatedly changing your direction. This is never a good idea. I remember all too well preparing for the championship three-course menu for the Culinary Olympics in 2004. We went through an intense development stage and had many practice runs before we asked advisors to come and watch us in the kitchen and to taste our food. This gave us a chance to perfect the way we worked, correct our mistakes, and really streamline our techniques. It also helped us to ensure that we were executing the basics and fundamentals properly.

There were some obstacles, however. We debated whether or not to use a savory tuile we developed, and how to lay out the finished plate itself. As team captain, the call was mine to make. I listened to the observations and suggestions from the advisors. I factored in the comments from the team chefs. The next morning, we had one final session, during which we implemented some of the comments from our advisors; but we also stuck with some things we felt strongly about, especially the tuile. Similarly, when reviewing our final pastry program a few weeks before departure for the competition, I felt strongly that there was too much chocolate on the petits fours program. Again, after much debate, I had to make the call, which was to reduce the chocolate.

At the end of the day, you, too, will have to make the final call on your food. Listen carefully and respectfully to all feedback, weigh it, and then make an educated decision. If you receive advice from an experienced judge, of course you should give his or her comments greater weight. Or if you are part of a team, and the captain advises strongly to change something, do so. But don't forget to trust your instincts—go with your gut, as they say.

 ## CONCLUSION

As in life, success in culinary competitions is never an accident: it is the result of commitment, intention, dedicated effort, clearly defined goals and objectives, intelligent direction, and skillful execution. In short, practice and hard work are the main ingredients in the recipe for success.

CHAPTER

6

Presentation

Presentation in the culinary sense refers to the balance, contrast, and visual impact of a plate of food that has been cooked and served. Presentation is, of course, an important aspect in the process of planning your program for a competition. How you develop your menu, design the placement of food on your platters and plates, and display the finished work all are factors used by the judges to assign point values to your program. Under the scrutiny of judges, a plate of hot food or a cold platter that looks overcooked, unappetizing, or poorly arranged will fare badly; whereas a plate or platter on which the food has a balanced presentation—some height and depth and fresh flavorful colors that harmonize naturally—will, obviously, win the approval of the judges—and valuable points for you, the competitor.

Simply put, presentation is important to the culinary tradition because people, including judges, "eat with their eyes" first. Presented with an appetizing plate of food that smells delicious, looks as good as it smells, and clearly demonstrates proper cooking methods will be irresistible to anyone, customers and judges alike.

UNDERSTANDING THE IMPORTANCE OF PRESENTATION IN CULINARY COMPETITIONS

How much weight does presentation carry in a culinary competition? In the cold food category, it is, simply, all you have; it's the whole show. In the hot food categories, its importance is less clear-cut, but to say it sets the tone for the judges conveys its impact. People say, "It's important to make a good first impression," but usually they say it in the context of presenting oneself—for a job interview, in a social situation, and so on. Well, in a culinary competition, your food must also make a good first impression, and that is the role of presentation.

There are four factors that comprise judging criteria for presentation:

- Overall look of the piece—the final display
- Creativity behind the display
- Workmanship to produce the food
- Composition—balance, color, and harmony

Judges also look for these more specific characteristics in a masterful presentation:

- **Consistency:** Do all the food courses look appetizing? Are they displayed in a simple yet elegant style?
- **Smell stimulation:** Is the food presented properly and served so that the aromas tantalize the nose, in turn stimulating the other senses?
- **Visual stimulation:** Can judges tell just by looking at it how flavorful the food is? In a hot-food-presented-cold competition, can you imitate the professional cooking procedures behind the presentation? Does just looking at the food make people want to "dig in?"
- **Craftsmanship:** Is the plate arranged in an appetizing style that says "a skilled craftsman prepared this presentation." Judges (who are, after all, people like you and me) love to see, smell, and taste delicious food presented plainly and simply.

 LEARNING TO PRESENT

So how does a cook or chef learn to be an effective presenter? For starters, by asking—and answering—the right questions:

- What am I trying to achieve?
- How can I accomplish this presentation in the time allotted?

PRESENTATION DEVELOPMENT CHECKLIST

A good way to approach food presentation is by remembering the acronym SCHIFT, which stands for *shape, color, height, items, flavor,* and *texture.* Here are some brief guidelines for each:

Shape. Avoid contrived food shapes. This can be accomplished by using a combination of sliced, molded, and loose and whole food items.

Color. Use a combination of earthtones and naturally vibrant colors. Usually, compatible flavors provide an exciting combination of natural colors.

Height. Incorporate the natural shape of food to provide varied, but not extreme, heights. This will enhance the *flow* of food on the plate.

Items. Choose food items based on practicality, portion size, number of other items on the plate, along with degree of preparation difficulty.

Flavor. This is the single *most important* factor. Use only fresh, compatible flavors, to enhance your presentation naturally.

Texture. To achieve a variety of textures, vary your cooking methods and apply different cuts to your vegetables to create variation.

- How can I showcase my food in an eye-pleasing manner?
- How can I avoid presentations that "go overboard" and are difficult for the judges to serve and eat?

The best way to proceed is to use diagrams. Draw out your concepts and see if they first "work on paper." Alongside the diagrams list your ingredients for review. Keep challenging yourself: ask why, if, and how.

The next step is the same for every other aspect of preparing for a competition: practice, practice, practice:

- Use the right equipment to finish your food—a burr mixer, squeeze bottle, palette knife, brush, foam gun. Proper tools yield professional results.
- Follow through on your concept, and focus on presenting food that does not detract from the original concepts.
- Make sure your professional cooking methods are apparent, whether in a cold or hot food display. Offer something special, a signature item that will set you apart from other chefs. Just make sure it is reasonable.

Let me share with you an example from my experience with ACF Culinary Team USA 2004. We were searching for our signature item, that special something, to set us apart in the international arena. Our decision was to do a spinoff of a chicken dumpling, to develop a dumpling for our venison dish, which we planned to fill with braised neck meat. We also placed a savory tuile on some parsnip purée to bring our three components together, adding crispness to the process. The result was that our dish served a purpose, added flavor, and was visually stimulating to the judges. The result? We scored one of only four gold medals awarded that week and took the top honors in the hot food championship.

 GARNISHING: PUTTING THE FINISHING TOUCH ON PRESENTATION

When it comes to determining how to garnish food for presentational purposes, you must first identify whether the garnish is *functional* or *nonfunctional*. Table 6-1 defines a number of garnish categories and gives examples for all.

Functional Garnishes

In this category, the guideline to follow is simple: Use functional garnishes that make sense. What makes a sensible garnish? A garnish that:

- Adds texture or taste to the food (it may also add color, but that should not be its only purpose—see "Nonfunctional Garnishes," below).
- Serves a purpose, such as to add crispness for a contrasting texture, or an infused oil to add a hint of another complementary flavor.
- Harmonizes with the item it accompanies, yet does not distract from the focal point of the plate.

Nonfunctional Garnishes

A nonfunctional garnish is any item, edible or inedible, that does not contribute to the taste or texture of a dish, but serves only a decorative purpose, usually in the form of color. In general, a chef should avoid the use of nonfunctional garnishes on plates and platters. A good way to distinguish whether a garnish is functional or nonfunctional garnish is to ask yourself, "Does this serve any purpose?" If the answer is, "Only to provide color," chances are you have a nonfunctional garnish.

TABLE 6-1   Garnish Categories and Examples

Nonfunctional Garnishes	Appropriate Starch and/or Vegetable Garnishes	Breads or Bread Items, to Add Texture and Variety	Sauces Used as Garnish	Salad Components, to Add Variety and Color	Compotes, Chutneys, and Relishes, to Add Flavor, Contrast, and Color
Wedge or slice of orange placed on a plate of eggs (scrambled, fried, omelet, etc.) Wedge or crown of lemon on a dish served with sauce Leaves of lettuce used as underliners for hot food on hot plates Traditional sprig of parsley or watercress.* Orange, lemon, or lime "baskets." Tomato "roses" and apple "birds." Paper or foil frills.	Vegetables, sliced or shredded sweet potatoes Carrots Daikon Parsnips Potato pancakes Baked wontons Gaufrette potatoes	Pita triangles Olive bread Phyllo dough (horns or baskets) Baked flour tortilla triangles Baked corn tortilla strips	Honey mustard Potato saffron Red pepper vinaigrette Carrot ginger sauce	Jicama salad Three-onion salad Orange and red Belgian endive	Mango and lobster relish Seasonal fruit compote Dried fruit compotes Salsas Apple and pear chutney

*There are times, classically and traditionally, when either watercress or parsley is appropriate. For example, watercress can be used on a plate that contains a simple grilled or roasted item.

 UNDERSTANDING THE CONTEXT OF FOOD PRESENTATION

Putting a presentation all together requires a thorough understanding of the context—the interrelated conditions—relating to the food to be served. This section addresses the main contextual components of food presentation, some of which we've discussed previously. They are:

- Food selection
- Balance
- Color
- Cooking method
- Shape
- Texture
- Seasoning
- Layout

Food Selection

First, of course, is the selection of the food. You must consider both simple and complex types of food in the context of food preparation in both the development and presentation stages: for example, a perfectly grilled piece of fish (simple) teamed up with lobster potato croquette (complex).

Balance

The concept of balance incorporates many factors in food presentation. You will balance food presentation through the selection of food, by choosing complementary flavors, which harmonize with each other, as well as seasonings and food groups that complement each other. You must also prepare food using different but complementary cooking methods and arrange it on appropriate dinnerware in an appetizing presentation.

Color

Color, as explained earlier, is always important in food, but it plays a particularly important role in presentation. Color should always reinforce the freshness of your food and attest to quality of preparation. In most cases, when food has been properly prepared, with a focus on harmonizing flavor profiles, seasonality, and classic combinations, it will paint a colorful picture.

It's a good idea to incorporate a variety of colors—but always with a light touch. You don't want a "circus" effect. A guiding principle here is that foods that taste good together will naturally harmonize in color. Again, use proper cooking techniques, vegetables and sauces that have synergy with the main items, and functional garnishes (those that serve a purpose and add to the dish). The combination of earthtones and vibrant color is often a successful approach, though color will, of course, depend to some degree on seasonality of the various foods.

Just as cooking highlights color, color should highlight the cooking technique applied; for example:

- Caramelize, to achieve a glaze on the outside of a roast.
- Sauté, for an even brown color.
- Steam, to maintain fresh food color.
- Grill, to achieve proper grill marks and a caramelized crust.
- Poach, for a translucent, or opaque, appearance.

Cooking Method

It's always a good idea to implement different cooking techniques, as doing so will automatically add a variety of textures to the presentation of your food. You can avoid repetition by using such different yet compatible methods as:

- Roasted whole meat with poached sausage
- Baked crust or a purée with braised meats
- Deep-fried fish with steamed vegetables

Shape

The watchword here is to avoid combining similar shapes on the same plate. Likewise, avoid too many whole or stuffed vegetables or too many loose mixtures on the same plate.

Texture

As with shape, avoid combining too many similar textures on the same plate. Utilize purées, custards, fried or toasted items, and so on to provide different textures. The basic textures to work with are:

- Smooth
- Coarse
- Solid
- Soft

Seasonings

Avoid using the same herbs and spices to provide flavor in the various foods on the same plate. That is, do not put garlic, herbs, and shallots in everything if they will be served together. The flavors should be complementary, as mentioned earlier.

Layout

Layout is a balancing act of lines, shapes, and dimensionality; and it encompasses the concepts of service. To be effective, these aspects must relate to the overall continuity of the plate or platter. For example, if you have a platter with several strong lines working against one another, it will be uncomfortable to look at. By enhancing the three-dimensionality of the food, to give the impression of action or motion, you will add excitement to the look of the platter.

Natural shapes are ideal for providing dimensionality to a plate or platter layout, so that the whole platter becomes a centerpiece, and judges do not have to second-guess what food item(s) they are viewing.

SERVICEABILITY

In regard to layout, "serviceability" refers to the ease with which guests can serve themselves from the plate or the platter. The guests should not be forced to move one item around in order to reach another. This is a vital aspect of plate layout.

The layout on a plate or a platter should work as a cohesive unit; there should be unity among all the food being served, a harmony of ingredients and items on the plate. Look at the drawings in Figure 6-1: the food components on the left are distributed to all parts of the plate; though the plate is full, the presentation is not unified. In contrast, on the plate on the right-hand side, the components have been brought together in a way that imposes unity; it is a plate well put together. A judge (or a customer) will get the impression of a delicious combination of food working together.

A more contemporary approach to plating features the main item as the focal point, in the center, with the other items underneath or around it or scattered on the plate (see Figure 6-2). Here you can see the effect of the absence of unity compared with two different styles of plating that achieve unity and balance.

Figure 6-1
Unity
Comparison 1

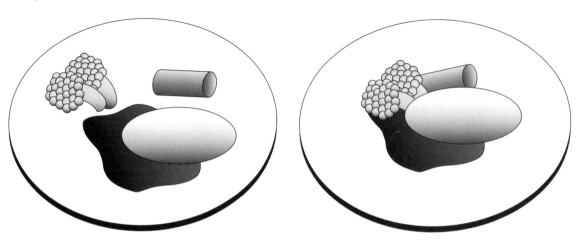

Figure 6-2
Unity
Comparison 2

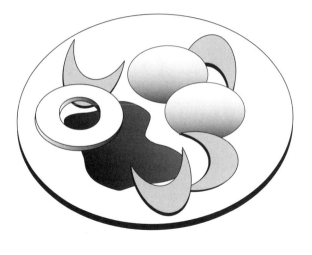

Haphazard, no unity

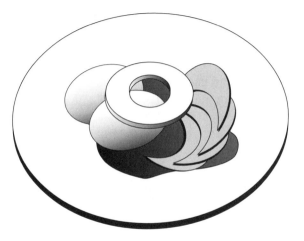

Unity and balance

Unity and balance
with center of the plate

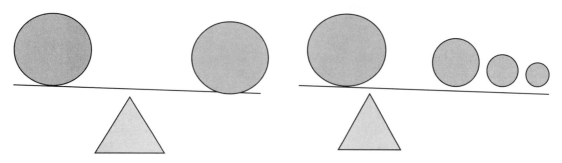

Figure 6-3
Symmetric
Balance (left)
and
Asymmetric
Balance (right)

FLOW

If the presentation is balanced and has unity, and the focal point is presented correctly, you will generate a positive flow of the food on a plate or platter, an important feature of layout. A *symmetric*, or stagnant, balance will neither flow nor create visual excitement; whereas an asymmetric balance will create synergy and a positive flow that is pleasing to the eye (see Figure 6-3).

When the presentation is not unified, it is impossible to form a pleasing pathway for the eye to follow; therefore, no flow is evident. And when a presentation is not unified, there is no strong focal point. This focal point is the necessary starting point from which the flow should emanate. A focal point or strong line can help you design a presentation that flows yet links the whole presentation.

Important to a successful presentation is the understanding and development of "strong" or "clean" lines. A strong line is one that makes a powerful statement of direction and lays a foundation around which to build your platter or plate presentation. The strong line shown in Figure 6-4 will convey a sense of freshness, strength, structure, and direction. The weak line in the

Figure 6-4
Strong and
Weak Lines 1

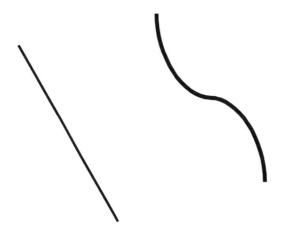

Figure 6-5
Strong and
Weak Lines 2

same figure indicates weakness, poor structure, and lack of definite direction. Strong clean lines are enhanced by the execution and good craftsmanship in the areas of shaping, cooking, slicing, frontal views, and sequencing. To enforce the strong-line concept, notice in Figure 6-5 how to build around the strong line, to generate flow and harmony; then notice how the weak line does just the opposite.

CONCLUSION

Remember, good food, whether hot or cold, is a combination of fresh ingredients prepared in the proper way with uncomplicated layers of harmonizing flavors. Sound combinations usually have their roots in ethnicity, regionality, or seasonality. You will need a solid understanding of how to build flavor profiles in order to present them with style.

CHAPTER

7

Culinary Techniques and Fundamentals in Garde Manger and Pastry

In any culinary competition you enter, you will be judged on your skill set, and to measure up you must be able to perform to a very high standard. In the cold food category, in particular, it is paramount that you be able to execute knife cuts masterfully and to demonstrate competency in all the fundamentals, because the visual effect and display of your food is all the judges have to evaluate.

The cold food arena is where a cook or chef defines him- or herself as a top craftsperson in the field of cookery. The skill and precision required for slicing, carving, and shaping, to produce an elegant and flawless presentation, is heavily weighted in your final score. Uneven, jagged slices will leave your presentation with an unfinished look, one that implies underdeveloped knife skills. Without honing these basic skills, you will fail to achieve your goal of displaying award-winning food, platters, and plates. Practice is essential, otherwise, you will never perfect this skill, which is so important as a culinarian.

FINE-TUNING THE CRAFT

My friend and colleague Chef Brad Barnes, who is at The American Culinary Federation, says there is a fine line between craftsmanship and the correct execution of the fundamental cooking processes and skill sets. What he means is that craftsmanship refers more to subtle well-practiced skills that a chef develops over time. Whether it is the smooth and quick butchery of a whole pig, the picture-perfect slicing of a torte, or the ability to cut a carrot into a brunoise, it is time, practice, and attention to detail that ultimately mark the difference between a craftsman and a technician.

Though it is true that many celebrated craftsmen and -women are blessed with natural capabilities, it is also true that the necessary skills can be taught/learned; all it takes is commitment to practice. It is only after working, for example, as a prep cook in a top hotel for six months, and preparing pounds of tourné vegetables every day for the hot kitchen that such a skill becomes second nature. In most cases, based on my experience, I would say that craftsmanship is not born, but bred of training and practice; it reflects what we do repeatedly.

Craftsmanship must become an intrinsic component of your competition toolkit. It is the skills of your hands, working in conjunction with the knowledge in your head: the way you cut a vegetable, smoothly remove the flesh from a fish, the single motion with which you peel a shrimp, or how you slice a perfectly cooked roast. These are the processes that require much practice and repetition in order to do them proficiently to receive accolades from the judges. Without craftsmanship you will find little success in the competition arena.

Whether you are competing individually or as part of a team, in international or national competitions, you will be expected to display a very high level of craftsmanship; where this is lacking, you will lose points. That said, expectations do vary based on professional status: a student will not, for example, be expected to perform at the same level as a Certified Master Chef.

CRAFTING IN THE COLD: SLICING AND GLAZING

As mentioned above, it is in the cold food category that culinary craftsmanship is the most apparent to the judges: it is what makes a platter or cold food display stand out—one on which each garnish, though sliced by hand, will have the look of precision machine work; one on which each element of a centerpiece comes to life. Two skill sets are necessary to reach that level of achievement: slicing and glazing. You must be able to execute these processes like a culinary craftsman in order to succeed.

You will, for example, be expected to produce a well-crafted cut such as a julienne, brunoise or tourné on your platter, whether for a salad or a hot food plate displayed cold; you will be expected to produce garnishes, sauces, and inlays so well a judge will have to look twice to believe they were hand-crafted.

Slicing the Right Way

For all its importance in the culinary arts, knife skills are a discipline that is too often neglected in the practice and preparation of food. Sad to say, I have seen too many times in competition a chef place on the cutting board a terrine or pâté, over which he or she has slaved the night before, and slice this work of art into uneven portions, of different thicknesses. This kind of mistake is irreversible; the poorly cut terrine or pâté is what the judges will see and remember.

The correct knife for the job, sharpened properly, and wielded correctly are the three components of the proper slicing technique. All you will produce with a dull knife and improper slicing motions is poorly presented food. Choosing the right knife for the job is not, however, always easy, as today there are many to choose from. Some of these are shown in Figure 7-1. From top to bottom you see a beveled chef's knife, a serrated chef's slicer, a straight-edge slicer, a beveled slicer, and a smoked salmon slicer.

Once you have the right knife in hand, it is imperative that you pay attention to proper technique, which is detailed below.

PROPER SLICING TECHNIQUE

1. Choose a worktable of a comfortable height, preferably three to four inches below your waist (see Figure 7-2). Clean the table well, then place a damp towel under the dry cutting board to help keep it in place. I recommend that you use a clean plastic or wooden cutting board.
2. Place a clean dry towel for your knives on the side of the board opposite the hand you use for slicing. Place the knives and other tools on the towel with the edges pointing *away* from you.
3. Set up a bain-marie for dipping the knife blade prior to slicing. This ensures a smoother stroke.
4. Using a 12-inch side-serrated or beveled slicing knife, slice away from yourself using a smooth continuous motion (see Figure 7-3). Then draw the blade back toward yourself, keep-

Figure 7–1
Types of Knives

ing the knife level. Do not saw the food. While slicing, keep the product wrapped in plastic to help keep the cuts smooth and intact.

5. With the tip of the knife, place the slice on a tray covered with plastic wrap and resting above ice to keep the product cool (see Figure 7-4). Lay the first slice at the farthest edge of the tray and work toward yourself so you don't have to lean over the sliced pieces.

SEQUENCE, NUMBER, AND DIRECTION OF SLICES

Three other important aspects of slicing that you must focus on are *sequence,* *number,* and *direction* of slices.

The guiding principle for sequencing is to display the slices in the same order you sliced them. This will ensure the consistent progression of any particular pattern in the item. For example, the natural marbling in a piece of meat or the changing size of a turkey, duck, or chicken breast will naturally create a

Figure 7–2
Optimum Height of a Worktable

strong line, unless you display the slices out of sequence or cut them unevenly (see Figure 7-5). Similarly, guard against "reversing" one or more slices when shingling a line of slices, as this will disrupt the flow of the line, weakening that line and making for a sloppy presentation. In Figure 7-6 you can see that the item on the left is in sequence; the item on the right is out of sequence.

Why is the number of slices important? Because it will affect service time, the temperature of the food, and the quality of the presentation.

And in terms of presentation, how you slice may dictate how you ultimately display the food. For example, a slice of New York strip sirloin over braised short ribs may make sense and be a plus in the plate presentation. A combination plate does not need a full steak; the slices can also go over the braised pulled meat to enhance the presentation. Even in this situation or in a large banquet, proper slice sequence will enhance the presentation.

Figure 7–3
Proper Way to
Slice

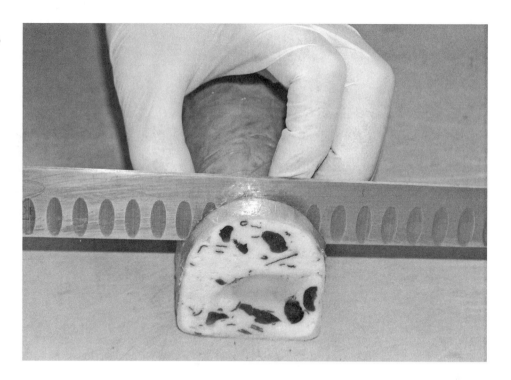

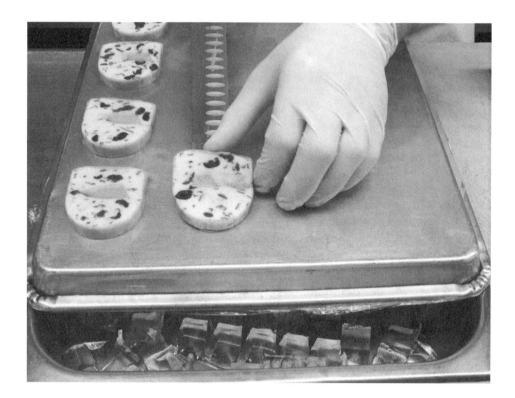

Figure 7–4
Placing the
Slice on the
Tray

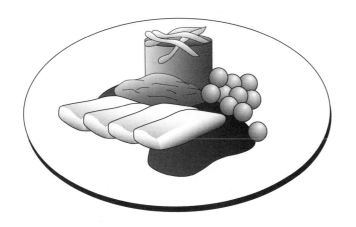

Figure 7–5
Arrangement and Sequencing

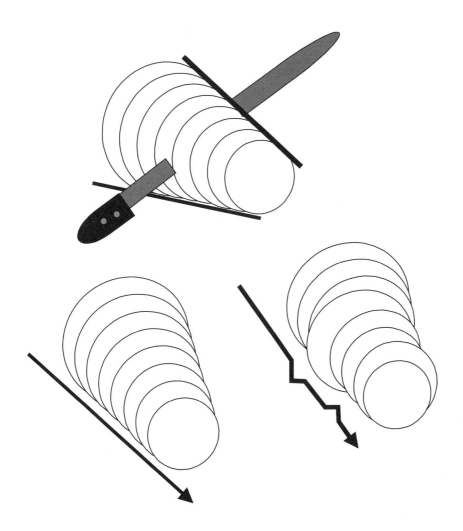

Figure 7–6
Slicing in Sequence.
Left: Proper Sequence;
Right: Improper Sequence

Figure 7–7
The Direction
of Slices.
Left: Proper
Arrangement;
Right: Improper
Arrangement

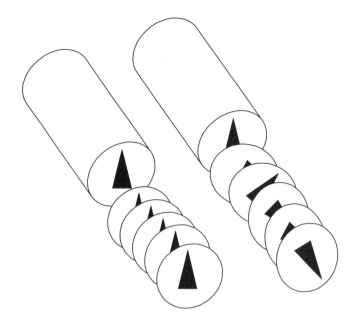

Finally, you must pay attention to the direction of slices. When slicing a roast, chicken breast, or terrine, each slice must be placed with the "outside" face up. This practice ensures that any inlay or garnish on the face of the gross piece will be displayed precisely on the presentation face of the slice. In Figure 7-7, note that the terrine on the left shows the proper arrangement of slices from the terrine; the garnish is all in the proper direction just like the gross piece. The one on the right shows the slices in reverse and out of sync, which results in a poor presentation and weak lines.

Glazing

Applying aspic or gelatin to food for glazing requires first that you follow recipes accurately and execute with a high degree of skill to produce consistent high-quality products. As in all aspects of food production, product quality is key—in this case, the gelatin and the quality of the water. Purchase a quality gelatin, such as Grayslake Gelatin or HACO Swiss, and use bottled or filtered water.

To prepare the gelatin, first gather the proper tools and lay them so that they are easily accessible throughout the glazing process. Weigh the gelatin and measure the water using the ratios shown in Table 7-1. Then follow the steps in the list below.

TABLE 7-1   Ratios for Preparing Gelatin for Glazing

For General Glazing	For Medium Glazing	Glazing for Special Circumstances*
16 oz. gelatin	12 oz. gelatin	8 oz. gelatin
1 gal. cold water	1 gal. cold water	1 gal. cold water

*Only highly skilled chefs should use this ratio, where there is consistently cool weather and when a very clear and moist end product is desired.

PREPARING GELATIN

1. Pour water into a very clean and dry stainless-steel bain-marie or similar container.
2. Slowly pour the gelatin over the water while gently stirring. Do not let foam or bubbles emerge, which will have to be removed later.
3. Let the gelatin "bloom," or soften, for at least 30 minutes.
4. Place the container in a large pot and pour hot water around it. Place on stove and heat water until it reaches 160°F. While the gelatin is melting and begins to form aspic, do not let the mixture boil or overheat; 95°F to 110°F is ideal.
5. When all the gelatin has melted and the aspic is crystal clear, remove the container and cool the aspic to between 85°F and 95°F.

The gelatin is now ready for the glazing of your food. For that purpose, gather the glazing tools listed in Table 7-2.

GELATIN CONTENT

The amount of gelatin used in aspics may exceed normal quantities but not to the extent that the presentation is dependent on the extra gelatin content.

TABLE 7-2   Glazing Tools

Thermometer	Sanding block
Sterno	Large glass bowls
Bain-marie to put tools in with hot water	Wire mesh aspic dippers (see Figure 7-8)
Cheesecloth and strainer, for removing particles from aspic	Cutting board
Sufficient 4x8-inch plastic-wrapped floral-quality Styrofoam blocks for toothpicked vegetables and small food items	Plastic wrap
Rectangular chafing dish with perforated pan	Paper towels
Gloves	Bamboo skewers
Tweezers	Glazing dipper utensils
Small spatula	Small pallet knife
Terrycloth towels	Hotel pans with ice
Plastic-wrapped Plexiglas or cafeteria trays (half-sheet pan size)	Quality wide and small brushes

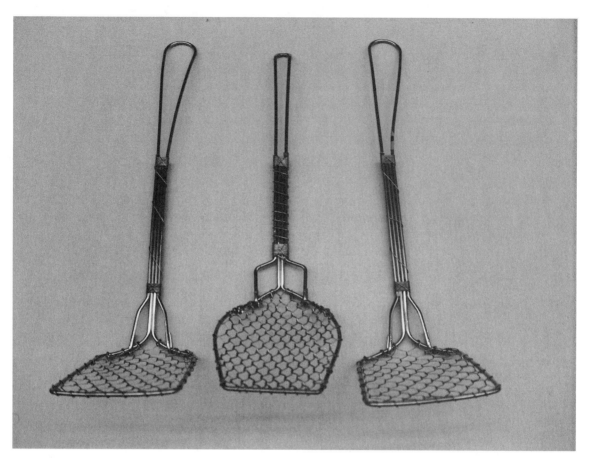

Figure 7–8
Glazing Tools

Set up your tray as shown in Figure 7-9, then follow the steps in the glazing procedure:

GLAZING PROCEDURE

1. Place your slices in order on a plastic-wrapped tray. Brush a first coat of gelatin on all pieces to be glazed (see Figure 7-10).
2. For seasoned hot food or marinated cold food, glaze the vegetables and season as needed with herbs, spices, shallots, and so on while first coat is still wet. Once a vegetable or starch has been seasoned, apply two more coats and chill for at least one hour.
3. Wait a minimum of 30 minutes between coats (patience is the key here), to allow the product to reach 40°F to 45°F degrees. Store all glazed pieces in a closed cabinet in the walk-in to avoid any air movement.

Figure 7–9
Tray Set-up

When they have reached the proper temperature and you are ready to start dipping, follow this procedure:

DIPPING PROCEDURE
1. Set up a chafing dish with 1 inch of hot water, a perforated 2-inch pan, and several layers of damp terrycloth toweling.
2. Light the Sterno and cover the chafer; allow the water to heat and warm the towel.
3. Line a strainer with cheesecloth and, during the glazing process, carefully strain the aspic through cheesecloth with a ladle (as you would consommé) to remove any accumulated bits of food and particles from the aspic that could result in an undesirable coating. *Do not* use the same bowl of gelatin for red meats, fish, and so on.

Figure 7–10
Brush Pieces for
First Coat

DIFFERENT FOOD, DIFFERENT GLAZING

There are several types of glazing procedures for different types of food:

- For smaller, thicker pieces such as tourné vegetables, beans, tomato slices, and the like, skewer with toothpicks. Remember to skewer long products at an angle or lay them flat to produce a natural look.

- Green and yellow vegetables need an additional coat of gelatin, as they will absorb the first coat or lose the last coat between finishes and display time. Items such as green beans and asparagus also absorb more aspic than other items.

- Foods that contain dough, such as pie wedges, pâté en croute, and barquettes, require that you use a good-quality, soft-bristle brush to paint a coat of aspic on the nondough portion of the food. (The dough portion of the food should remain unglazed.) Brush only once, in one direction, and then turn the brush to another area. Repeated brushing will result in streaks or roughness.

As with other foods, cool thoroughly before applying another coat.

4. Begin to dip the foods. You can do this individually (see Figure 7-11) or in quantity; for the latter, place the food in the aforementioned foam block. This method saves time and, with practice, results in a very clean and consistent appearance.

5. Take your brushed slices and head piece and start to work in the largest quantities possible. For example, dip 10, not two or three, slices of one galantine at a time, in order, at a smooth pace. The food will stay cold and glazing will proceed quickly.

6. Glaze food slices using a specialized dipping tool. Wearing rubber gloves, lift the slice using the dipping tool and a palette knife. Dip the slice in aspic, making sure all sides receive an even coating.

7. Place the slice on a prepared sheet pan, sliding it off the dipping tool using a palette knife. With care you should not have any runoff or drips to clean later. This will save valuable time.

Figure 7–11
Dipping Your Slices

TIP

When doing the first and second coats, hold glazing tools as level as possible to ensure even coating. Then blot quickly so as not to remove too much aspic against the warm towel (see Figure 7-12).

When you have glazed all pieces, slices, head pieces, and vegetables, let them chill for at least an hour before attempting to clean them. Then follow the cleaning procedure, which follows.

CLEANING PROCEDURE

1. Wearing rubber gloves, take each piece and "polish" along the side of a warm chafing dish. Avoid any contact with heat rising up from the Sterno under the chafing dish, as this will bring the temperature of each piece down and will start the deterioration of the glazing effect.
2. Using a warm knife, trim off any excess aspic and remove any bubbles by lightly applying the knife to the food. Place the cleaned

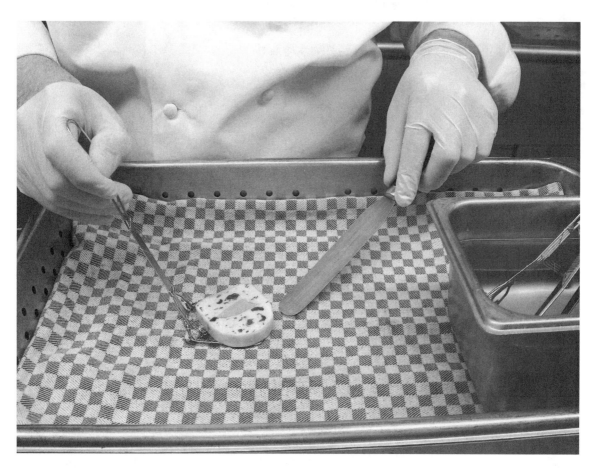

Figure 7–12
Blotting Slice

ASPICS FOR SALADS

For salads, you prepare aspics by adding the ingredients that you would use in vinaigrette dressing—herbs, mustard, garlic, pepper vinegar, and so on—directly into the aspic. The one exception is oil; oil will ruin aspic. Make sure your greens are dry, crisp, and very cool—about 38°F—then dip them into the aspic vinaigrette, drain well, and lay on a prepared sheet pan. If the ends do not coat as well as the body, brush them with aspic after you have completed glazing. Do not overdip salad greens or they will take on a thick appearance that is unappealing.

For salads on a buffet layout and on platters such as wild mushroom salad, mixed vegetable slaw, mixed seafood, and salads that have been shredded, mix the proper portion of salad as it will appear on the platter. With tweezers dip and place on a template designed for the layout onto the platter. Brush any additional glazing to highlight. Don't forget to season the salad.

pieces in 2- or 4-inch pans, arranging them by food type and the order in which they will be used (see Figure 7-13).

3. Match up all the items required to complete a buffet platter, plate, or hot platter. Cover the pans with plastic to prevent drying, and keep them chilled until time for setup.

A number of other tips for glazing and cleaning will help you master this craft:

- Coordinate all glazed components on racks in sequence.
- Paint all sauces with a thin coat of aspic after plate setup to prevent dryness and to produce a nice sheen.
- When possible, plate up in a refrigerated environment.
- When cleaning, cover a stainless-steel table with plastic wrap or a clean white tablecloth. Set up chafing dish with warm water just touching the perforated pan. Line the perforated pan with two clean, hot, wet towels.
- Have one bowl of cold and one bowl of hot water ready for use.
- Place two spatulas and two palette knifes at each station.
- Line hotel pans with plastic wrap to put finished, cleaned pieces in.
- When ready for plate-up, line all pieces as they will appear on the platter in proper order from the head piece.

As you see, both skill and organization are important to achieving successful results in the glazing procedure; patience is the third essential factor in perfecting this craft.

Figure 7–13
Placing on Tray
in Sequence

 KEEPING YOUR EYE ON THE PRIZE

In addition to perfecting your craft skills, when you are preparing for a culinary competition, it helps to have some insight as to how the judges see things—as this may be very different from your viewpoint. This also comes with practice and repeated entries into various competitions.

In General

"Keeping your eye on the prize" is good advice, but only if you recognize that it means to maintain a focus on *all* that it takes to make a good impression on the judges, to never losing sight of the fundamentals: cleanliness, timeliness, attention to detail, demonstration of simple but yet well-executed methods of cookery. Identify your exhibits by their proper names, both on exhibition tables and on entry forms. And if you use classical terminology, remember, your preparation must follow the cooking rules that those terms imply.

The main criterion for judging all dishes is the recipe, or, for cold displays, the application, along with the table cards that provide a brief description of ingredients and methods of preparations. I've said this before, but it bears repeating: ingredients and garnishes must harmonize with the main part of the dish, in flavor, seasonality, and color, and conform to contemporary standards of nutritional balance. Avoid the use of unnecessary ingredients and garnishes and apply only practical, acceptable cooking methods. For example, judges regard dressing the rims of plates with herbs or spices as undesirable, as not contributing to the dish in any way.

NOTHING PERSONAL
No personal or business affiliation identification is allowed on the exhibits until the judging is completed.

The Meat of the Matter

If you are serving meat, make sure it is cooked properly (medium—that is, pink, so that no blood is drawn during glazing) and carved correctly and cleanly. Meat (and vegetable) juices will make a dish look unappetizing. Proper glazing, along with the proper cooking methods, will prevent this. As detailed above, serve meat slices with the carved surface facing upward and in the proper order. If you plan to use fruit to garnish meat, cut it into small pieces or slice it thinly; glaze it correctly. Again, the watchwords for garnishes are harmony and purpose.

All the Trimmings—Vegetables, Garnishes, Dressings

For vegetables, make sure you cut or turn them uniformly—here, too, you have an opportunity to display a high level of craftsmanship. Keep your garnishes, trimmings, and dressings fresh longer by cooking them so they remain firm to the touch; then glaze them with aspic as per the glazing guidelines given earlier in this chapter.

FRAMING THE PICTURE
Although judges do not evaluate table decorations as part of your score, a well-presented and attractive table will add to the high-quality image of your exhibit, so in a sense they do "count."

Up at the Plate—Arrangements and Decorations

Keep your plate arrangements and decorations practical yet appealing. Adhere to contemporary methods, and make sense of the food on the plate. In general, avoid all nonedible items.

Use proper plates and platters to display your hot or cold displays. Never place hot food presented cold on buffet platters or mirrored surfaces, only on ovenproof china or heatproof trays and dishes; likewise, do not serve food prepared hot on dishes glazed with aspic. Conversely, display dishes prepared hot but displayed cold glazed with aspic to keep them fresh; that said, be sure to emphasize the hot cookery aspect.

Other arrangement and decorative principles include the following:

- Place eggs on glass, porcelain, or on aspic-glazed dishes.
- Make plated portions proportional to the dish itself and the number of persons specified, per the guidelines.
- Fill sauce boats with enough sauce to ensure an equal amount per serving—between 1 to 2 ounces per serving—and glaze them on top to keep their appearance fresh.
- Use the right aspic for the product: clear aspic with fish, tan aspic with meat.
- In general, adjust portion weight according to the norms of accepted practice and nutritional balance.

You'll find a concise yet comprehensive listing of do's and don'ts in Table 7-3, and display guidelines for both hot and cold foods in Table 7-4.

Just Desserts

In this section we'll consider both a cold dessert platter and individual cold, plated desserts. But, first, some basic guidelines.

Steps to a Successful Pastry Display

1. Develop a theme (holiday, festive, etc.).
2. Choose your medium (bread, yeast-raised, chocolate, etc.).
3. Decide on varieties and portions (how many varieties and for how many portions).
4. Decide on a centerpiece, if required: functional or decorative, or both (see below).
5. Decide on the type of platter display you will use: silver platters, mirrored surfaces, plates; edible bases, trays, or plates made out of, for example, sugar or chocolate; fabric-covered boards or other types of display items.
6. Work out all details of display components:
   - ☐ Determine the size, color, texture, and shape of each item.
   - ☐ Decide on the size and shape of the centerpiece.
   - ☐ Produce other decorations (e.g., custom-made items that have to be prepared in advance).

TABLE 7-3   Competitor Do's and Don'ts

Focus On	Avoid
Numerical harmonizing of meat portions and garnishes	Use of inedible materials and items that do not serve a purpose to the display or food being presented
Respecting the character of the showpiece	Excessively thick glazing, sloppy glazing, or too little glazing
Achieving a natural, appetizing presentation that shows flavor	Decorating with parsley, watercress, long sticks of rosemary, and other gimmicks that serve no purpose
Proper presentation of sliced meats (arranged in order and size)	Cluttering the platters; having no defined strong line
Well-prepared food that shows high-quality craftsmanship	Cloudy aspic or aspic with bubbles
Methodology of cooking principles	Molded sculptures for which no molds were made
Ensuring that garde-manger food is used for cold displays, and that hot food looks and presents like hot food	Too many sculptures or too heavy a super-structure for sculptures
Creating menus that harmonize in flavor, show respect for proper cooking methods, and include seasonal profiles	Entering a previously judged piece
Platter and plate layouts that feature strong lines but offer sensible service to the customer	Identifying a display prior to judging
Following the guidelines and meeting or exceeding the category requirements	Serving food on the rim of the platter
Practicing the competition items ahead of time; tasting food during practice, especially for hot food competitions	Repetition in preparatory methods
Being original; expressing new ideas that are sensible but add something new	Excessive use of food coloring or any unnatural colors
Practical portion sizes (including cost and nutritional considerations)	Use of plastic ornaments, flowers, etc.
Proper color, presentation, and flavor synergy of food	Use of tarnished silver, dirty copper, dirty china, and items that show wear and tear; use of unsuitable serving dishes
Properly cooked meats, fish, poultry, and accoutrements	Presenting hot food on mirrored surfaces
Precisely cut vegetables that are cooked and seasoned correctly and complement the dish	Overdressing or overdecorating the presentation table
Nutritional quality, variety, balance, moderation	Use of wineglasses and/or silverware
Displaying a variety of skills and cookery methods	Copying award-winning platters or plates, thus showing no originality
Fusion of other ethnic flavor profiles, used correctly and sensibly	
In pastry, a variety of flavors and skills (Do not, for example, feature all chocolate desserts or pastries; provide an option for the customer/judge who may not like, or is allergic to, chocolate.)	Serving hot food on cold plates and serving cold hot food
	Cooking fusion cuisine without fully mastering it or understanding how the flavors work
	Bringing too many tools and gimmicks into the hot kitchen

TABLE 7-4   Proper Display of Cold and Hot Food

Display Cold Food On	Display Hot Food On
Silver trays and platters	Lined copper dishes
Stainless steel	Stainless-steel platters
Mirrors	Earthenware dishes (ovenproof)
Formica	Dinner plates (china, porcelain, and ceramic)
Polished wood	Polished or coated pewter
China plates or platters	Silver platters
Copper	Any nonporous surface
Any other approved food surface	

    ☐ Confirm that all the food items (seasonal items) you need will be available at show time.

7. Develop a layout of the display:

    ☐ Make templates of items and centerpiece (correct size).

    ☐ Use templates to develop lines, flow, proportions, and placement of centerpiece on your display (this will prevent problems or "surprises" during setup).

8. Organize your work time:

    ☐ Develop a detailed schedule (weekly, then daily as it gets closer to competition date).

    ☐ Set priorities and deadlines: what gets done first and by when.

    ☐ Practice well ahead of time, and be sure you know how much time it takes to prepare each item.

    ☐ Gather necessary equipment (molds, cutters, dishes, etc.).

    ☐ Allow time to address unforeseen problems, adjustments, or changes.

And, finally, as for hot food, make sure all your ingredients and garnishes harmonize with the main theme of the display, and demonstrate proper techniques and accepted methods of preparation throughout the display.

COLD DESSERT PLATTER

A cold dessert platter, which is usually designed to serve 8 to 10 portions, depending on the size of the serving tray it will be displayed on, should include a main dessert item, which can be made up of any number of dessert mediums. The most common are Bavarian creams, mousses, and flavored creams, which are usually molded or filled into a "container" typically fashioned out of chocolate marzipan, hippen masse, tuile, and other delectables. Other components of the main dessert might include chocolate ornament hippen masse garnishes or glazed fruit. Sauces and cookies act as accompaniments to the main dessert.

A centerpiece, either decorative or functional, will help carry the theme of the platter (more on centerpieces below). Possible platter themes include:

Holiday: Easter, Christmas, Valentine's Day

Festive: Birthday, children's theme, celebrations, countries

Seasonal: Fall (harvest), spring, winter

Fantasy: Musical, nature, fruit or wine

As an example, an assorted chocolates/praline platter would include 6 varieties, 8 to 10 portions of each, to include a number of basic preparations such as ganaches, liquor candies, gelees, marzipan centers, nougat (gianduga), and fondants.

Similarly, a petits fours glacé display would also include 6 varieties, 8 to 10 portions of each, covered with a coating, usually a thin layer of fondant icing. The cake and filling will vary according to taste, as will the garnish or decoration. A cookie display would include 6 varieties, 8 to 10 portions of each of a number of different types of cookies or biscuits from macaroon mix, hippen masse, tuile, and icebox cookies, and various cookie doughs.

INDIVIDUAL COLD, PLATED DESSERTS

For this type of display, include four different desserts prepared so that each one represents an individual portion of dessert. The makeup of each plate should be similar to that of the makeup of a cold dessert platter, discussed above: there should be the main dessert theme item, its components, and any accompaniments (sauces, cookies, etc.) to round off the presentation.

TIP

It's a good idea to include different methods of preparation for each plate to avoid having too many similar-looking desserts and to show off your range of skills.

Centerpieces for Dessert Platters

A centerpiece of some type is required in order to enhance the dessert items on a cold dessert platter. The media most commonly used to produce pastry centerpieces are: chocolate, krokant, pastillage, royal icing, sugar (pulled, poured, blown, or rock), and marzipan.

There are three primary considerations when designing a centerpiece, *size, time,* and *purpose* (functional or decorative or both):

1. **Size:** When a centerpiece is being used to highlight the product on any platter, whether it is a food or dessert platter, it should never be so large that it overpowers or overshadows the items being served.

Always design the centerpiece according to the platter size as well. A centerpiece too large or small on the wrong-size platter will either take up too much space or lose its impact. The centerpiece must also reflect the theme and show a variety of skills.

2. **Time:** The time you need to produce a quality centerpiece depends on five factors: *size of the item, degree of difficulty, your skill level,* and *material and composition of the item(s).* Can you make it ahead of time or does it have to be made at the last minute? For example, pastillage items may need more time than a pulled sugar centerpiece.

3. **Functional or decorative:** Depending on a platter design, a centerpiece may be described as either functional or decorative or both. Functional centerpieces, in addition to being decorative, can serve a number of different functions, such as to be an intricate part of the service. Decorative centerpieces function only to highlight or enhance the food being presented with it.

Here are some examples:

■ **Chocolate candy box on a chocolate platter:** This would be considered both decorative and functional. It would hold some of the chocolates; and at the end of the buffet, the box could be used for a table centerpiece, or put on display with chocolates inside.

■ **Wine bucket made from chocolate on a dessert platter:** Again, both decorative and functional, as it could be used to hold the sauce for the platter, as well as tie into the theme and other items on the platter, such as wine cream Bavarian. It might also be the focal point of the platter to highlight the theme for the judges.

■ **Pulled sugar flower basket:** This is a purely decorative centerpiece since the basket itself would not have any function other than to enhance the platter.

To keep pace with the constant changes in our industry, today's pastry chef faces the challenge of developing more efficient, simplified ways of producing high-quality results, often with less staff and limited space. For this reason, it is important that you also consider the practicality of a centerpiece. Even well-thought-out designs can be impractical to produce, so it is important to understand their makeup and assembly. In this regard, ask yourself:

■ Is the size of the centerpiece in proper proportion to the platter and its contents?

■ Does the centerpiece have a service function? If not, can it be modified to do so, making it more practical to produce? Develop a layout of the display. Make templates of items and centerpiece (actual size). Use the templates to determine lines, flow, proportions, and placement of centerpiece on your display (this will prevent surprises later when setting up).

■ Is the most logical medium being used to produce the centerpiece?

■ Will it take longer to produce the centerpiece than it will to produce the food item it was meant to enhance?

■ Can the centerpiece be simplified or modified to make its production more efficient without sacrificing the quality of its workmanship?

■ Will climactic conditions (humidity, heat) or working conditions affect the practicality of the centerpiece?

CONCLUSION

My primary purpose in this chapter was to detail how and why culinary fundamentals and techniques are critical to your success in the culinary and pastry competition arena. Craftsmanship is achieved by constant training. To be a culinary professional, you must never waver in your quest for excellence and commitment to be the best.

Team USA
Contemporary Pastry
Plate: Raspberry Mousse,
Warm Tart with Ice
Cream, and Lemon
Chocolate Napoleon

Baker Peeling Apples, Marzipan
Sculpture, 2004 IKA.

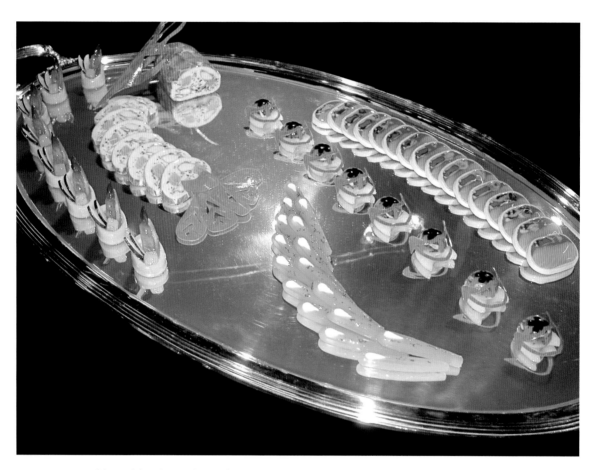

Team USA's Gold Medal Lobster Platter for Luxembourg—Chef Rich Rosendale, CC

Cured Roasted Salmon, Asparagus, Sea Bean Salad—Chef Dan Scannel, CMC, Team USA 2004

Diver Scallop with Truffle, Smoked Cod and Potato Cake, Corn Cream and Lobster Mousse

"Healthy Cuisine" Shrimp with Vegetable Spring Rolls and Tomato Foam—Chef Edward Leonard, CMC

Petits Fours Display
Culinary Classic
2003—Chef Patricia
Nash, Team USA
2004

Team USA's Trilogy
of Chocolate Hot
Kitchen Pastry
Culinary Classic
2003

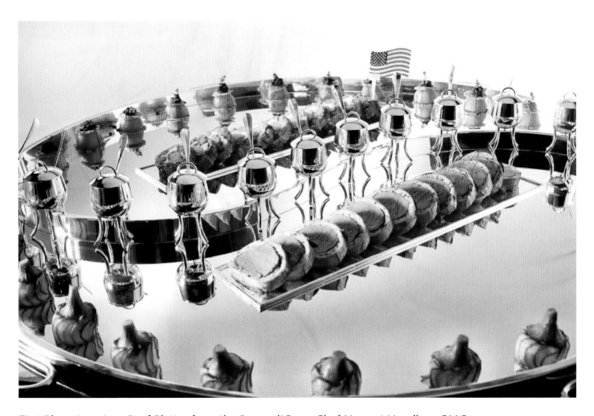

First Place American Beef Platter from the Bocus d'Ore—Chef Harmut Handkes, CMC

Restaurant Platter for Two: Crown Roast of Rabbit with Fall Vegetables—Chef Joachim Bucher, Team USA 2004

Finger Food of Rabbit Chops with Chutney—Chef Richard Rosendale, CC, Team USA 2004

Trilogy of Asparagus, Tempura, 12-hour Cooked Spears, and Foamy White Asparagus Soup—Chef Edward Leonard, CMC

Strategies for Success in Hot Food Competitions

When developing a menu for hot food competitions, the guiding principle is to take an organized, commonsense approach. You will have 20 minutes to finish and serve all your items to the judges, which leaves no room for error. That means you must consider, in advance, everything from top to bottom, from beginning to end. For starters, in the competition arena, you never know what kind of kitchen will await you: it could be anything from a kitchen in a school or a makeshift facility in a large hall. What is the size of the kitchen? What's its layout? How can you set up the flow of your workspace and the service space? What equipment will you need to prepare your menu? You'll also have to determine how many courses you will prepare, always maintaining a focus on quality. For example, if a fourth course is an option, first make sure you can prepare three to a high standard before you decide to add the fourth. Remember, only the successful execution of *all* courses will earn you points. In most cases, the courses will be a first plate or soup, a salad, a main plate with vegetable and starch, and an optional or requirement dessert.

Another critical consideration is degree of difficulty. You'll want to balance this; that is, don't make each item on your menu of a difficult nature to "show off." Be smart: recognize your limitations, both timewise and skill-wise. Review the self-evaluation checklist given earlier in the book. Then and only then, begin to develop your menu.

DEVELOPING A MENU

When developing a hot food menu for competition, it's okay to think outside the box and be creative, but keep it sensible and simple. Plan your menu around your skill base: if, for example, you've never made a consommé, do not attempt one in the competition kitchen; if you do not tourné well, do not tourné your vegetable or write this in your menu description. Next, draw or sketch your plate concepts and look at them to ensure they include all the items that make up a winning dish. (See the sidebar "More on Conceptual Design" for helpful hints on using drawings to formulate your ideas.) A good way to help you do this is to use what I call a "stimulation think chart" for your food and your concepts, shown in Figure 8-1. This will guide you as you look at what is available and think of new ways that it might be cooked, displayed, and so on. For each item, whether fish, beef, or vegetables, go down the list identifying texture, shape, form, flavor, and so on, as shown here:

COURSE

First plate, salad, main plate, side plate or dish

PORTION

Size and number

MODIFIERS

Texture: Leave whole; chop, grind, mince, purée; add egg or cream

Shape: Mold, roll-dice, slice and shingle, stack; filets or whole

Form: Cut in half lengthwise, crosswise, diagonally; wrap it in something (e.g., forcemeat, pastry, leaf vegetables, meat)

Temperature: Serve it hot, cold, or in between; rare, medium-rare

Flavor: Add seasonings, herbs, spices; marinades, brines; cure

Cooking method: Sauté, deep-fry, smoke-roast, broil, bake, poach, stew

OTHER ITEMS

Can you add flavor or texture (e.g., using vegetables, fruit, cream, fat, cheese, forcemeat, salpicon, duxelle, pastry, meat, fish, poultry)?

Stimulating Chart for Hot Food

Finfish	Shellfish	Vegetables
Course	Course	Course
Size	Size	Size
Modifiers	Modifiers	Modifiers
Texture?	Texture?	Texture?
Shape?	Shape?	Shape?
Form?	Form?	Form?
Temperature?	Temperature?	Temperature?
Flavor?	Flavor?	Flavor?
Cooking method?	Cooking method?	Cooking method?
Other items to build into dish or item?	Other items to build into dish or item?	Other items to build into dish or item?
Pork	**Beef**	**Veal**
Course	Course	Course
Size	Size	Size
Modifiers	Modifiers	Modifiers
Texture?	Texture?	Texture?
Shape?	Shape?	Shape?
Form?	Form?	Form?
Temperature?	Temperature?	Temperature?
Flavor?	Flavor?	Flavor?
Cooking method?	Cooking method?	Cooking method?
Other items to build into dish or item	Other items to build into dish or item?	Other items to build into dish or item?
Poultry	**Game**	**Fruit, Groceries**
Course	Course	Course
Size	Size	Size
Modifiers	Modifiers	Modifiers
Texture?	Texture?	Texture?
Shape?	Shape?	Shape?
Form?	Form?	Form?
Temperature?	Temperature?	Temperature?
Flavor?	Flavor?	Flavor?
Cooking method?	Cooking method?	Cooking method?
Other items to build into dish or item?	Other items to build into dish or item?	Other items to build into dish or item?

Figure 8-1
Stimulating Chart for Hot Food

Can you make your portions smaller or larger?

Is there an alternative food item you can use instead, such as pairing your meat with a certain vegetable or starch component?

Can it serve other uses (e.g., the dessert chocolate perhaps used to flavor a sauce on the main plate)?

Can you add a practical garnish that adds texture, flavor, and serves a purpose to the dish you are presenting?

Next, go through this list of guidelines, which will help you define even more specifically what will and won't work for you and your menu:

- Balance items that can be prepped ahead of time against those that have to be prepared at the last moment. Do not pressure yourself into preparing too many items against the clock.
- Consider a cold preplated appetizer or salad as opposed to one that has to be assembled at service. The challenge here, however, is to ensure it holds well and has great flavor profiles to win you points.
- Resist the urge to use too many gimmicky items and be overcreative in an attempt to impress the judges. I'll say it again: well-cooked, properly plated and seasoned food that tastes great and demonstrates knowledge of cookery fundamentals will win every time.
- Don't put an item on the plate unless it serves a purpose in the presentation and, more importantly, in the eating experience.
- Vary textures, flavors, cooking techniques, seasonings.
- Avoid repetition in plating concepts. For example, sauce painting both the entree and dessert; or slicing, layering, and stacking everything.
- Honor seasonality. When Team USA went to Germany in October 2004, we took care to feature the flavors of fall and autumn, so that the products we used reflected the time of year, which in turn showed respect for food product and demonstrated common sense.

TIP
Make sure your food is TACT-ful, that it has Taste, Aroma, Color, and Texture.

Another critical concept I want to reiterate here—that of unity or harmony. Everything must work together, not only in each course but within the menu as a whole and together on a plate. After developing your dish, eat it yourself! Taste each item individually; then taste the combinations as one. You may find that your first course doesn't match well or doesn't harmonize with the main item or its accoutrements.

Tradition, too, is a concept to value in cooking for competitions. Traditional flavor combinations and foods are enjoyed by almost everyone, including judges. Pork and apples, for example, are two flavors that combine well and are widely accepted and enjoyed. You can still be creative, yet sensible, with that traditional duo. How about a roast pork with apple spaetzle? That would make a nice variation on a classic combination that the judges would recognize and identify with. Again, creative and sensible: words to cook—and win by.

That's a lot to think about, I know, but it will be easier to assimilate this information in the context of some actual menu exercises.

Exercise 1: Three-Course Luncheon Menu

First we will develop a three-course lunch menu for a luncheon competition, then draw the three courses to get a visual feel for our concept. This will serve as a foundation to develop our cooking strategy and action plan. The menu is shown below, and its components filled out using our stimulation chart in Figure 8-2.

THREE-COURSE LUNCHEON MENU

Brie Cheese Soup, with fennel croutons

Baked Fillet of Sea Bass, on piquant tomato sauce with aged balsamic vinegar and potato-olive tart

Painter's Palette of assorted sorbets with cookie paintbrush

Figure 8-2
Three-Course Luncheon Menu

Now look at the sketches for these three items, shown in Figures 8-3 through 8-7.

Fish: <u>Sea Bass</u>	Fruit, Starch, Cheeses <u>Brie Soup</u>	Pastry: <u>Sorbet w/ Cookie</u>
Course: <u>Main Plate</u>	Course: <u>First Plate</u>	Course: <u>Dessert, Third Plate</u>
Size: _____	Size:	Size:
Modifiers:	Modifiers:	Modifiers:
Texture: Baked, sautéed_____	Texture: Creamy, plus crisp Fennel Croutons	Texture: Soft, crispy, creamy
Shape: Fillet _____	Shape: Croutons oval	Shape: Palette, round
Form: Natural_____	Form: In bowl	Form: Set inside palette
Temperature: Served hot_____	Temperature: Hot	Temperature: Cold to room temperature
Flavor: Tart, spicy, sweet, salty____	Flavors: Brie cheese, truffle	Flavor: Fruity, sweet, tart, creamy, vanilla
Cooking method: Sauté, bake____	Cooking method: Cream soup	Cooking method: Bake, sorbet
Other items to build into dish or item:	Other items to build into dish or item:	Other items to build into dish or item:
Sweet balsamic drizzle	Lace with tomato oil and sprinkle with chopped chives	Chocolate garnish
Fried basil? Glazed cucumbers, garlic slivers in fish, squash ribbons		Variety of sauces

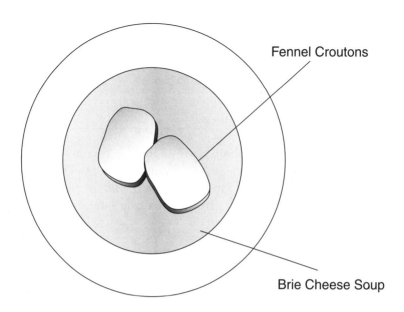

Fennel Croutons

Brie Cheese Soup

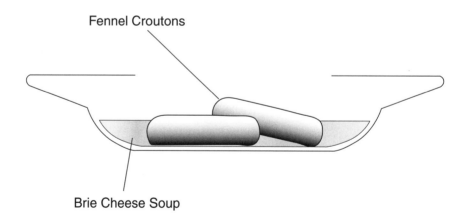

Fennel Croutons

Brie Cheese Soup

Figure 8-3
Brie Cheese Soup

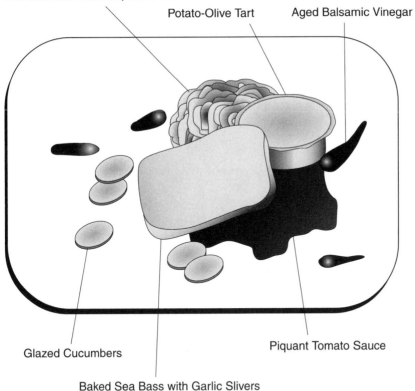

Zucchini and Yellow Squash Noodles

Potato-Olive Tart

Aged Balsamic Vinegar

Glazed Cucumbers

Piquant Tomato Sauce

Baked Sea Bass with Garlic Slivers

Figure 8-4
Baked Fillet of
Sea Bass (top)

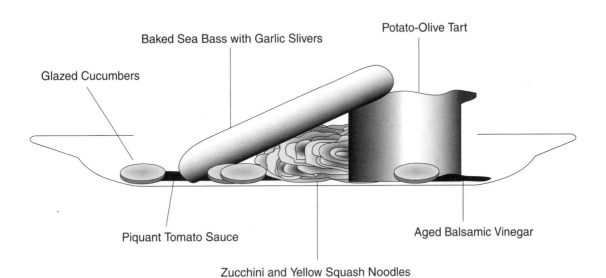

Baked Sea Bass with Garlic Slivers

Potato-Olive Tart

Glazed Cucumbers

Piquant Tomato Sauce

Aged Balsamic Vinegar

Zucchini and Yellow Squash Noodles

Figure 8-5
Baked Fillet Sea Bass (side)

95

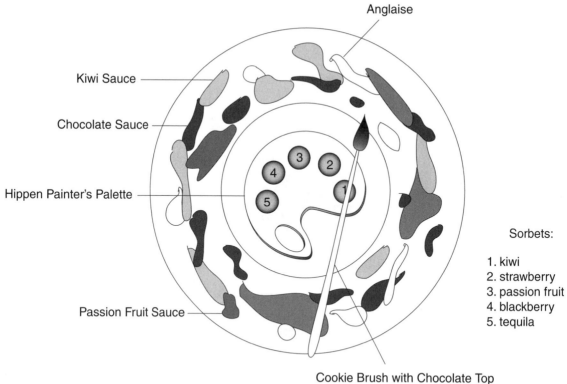

Figure 8-6
Painter's Palette (top)

Anglaise

Kiwi Sauce

Chocolate Sauce

Hippen Painter's Palette

Passion Fruit Sauce

Cookie Brush with Chocolate Top

Sorbets:

1. kiwi
2. strawberry
3. passion fruit
4. blackberry
5. tequila

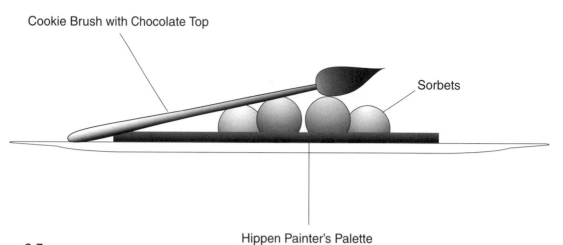

Figure 8-7
Painter's Palette (side)

Cookie Brush with Chocolate Top

Sorbets

Hippen Painter's Palette

MORE ON CONCEPTUAL DESIGN

Ever since I began to compete, and in particular as a member of Culinary Team USA, I have found it invaluable to go through a conceptual design stage—putting my ideas on paper. I strongly recommend you get into this habit. This does not mean you have to be an artist! The goal is to get you to more accurately visualize your plans. I think you'll find that, sometimes, an image may look good in your "mind's eye," but put on paper it doesn't "work." Nor do you even have to use paper; if you're more comfortable using a computer drawing program, do so. Find a way that works for you to create a visual picture that you can then turn into reality—with some work and adjustments, of course.

Figure 8-8
Template for
How to Get
Started

Name of Dish
Items

(continues)

Just be sure you write down/draw *all* the items on the plate, from garnish to sauce, as this will also assist you in determining whether you are headed in the right direction. Check and recheck the menu and its design for balance: protein versus starch and vegetables, proper sauces, garnishes, and so on. Think of the conceptual design stage as the step prior to getting behind the stove. Figure 8-8 gives you a template to get you started, and Figures 8-9 through 8-14 give you sample layouts to show you how this process works.

Figure 8-9
Beef Tenderloin

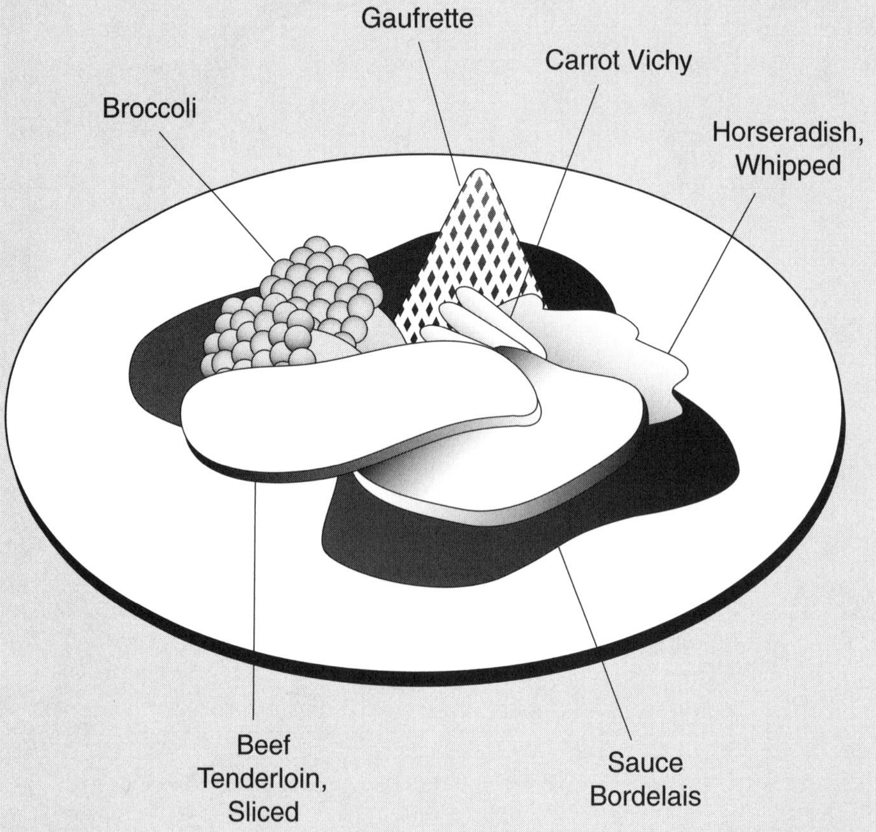

Gaufrette

Carrot Vichy

Broccoli

Horseradish, Whipped

Beef Tenderloin, Sliced

Sauce Bordelais

Figure 8-10
Vegetable
Mushroom
Napoleon

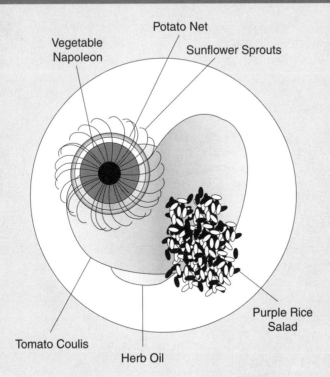

Vegetable
Napoleon

Potato Net

Sunflower Sprouts

Purple Rice
Salad

Tomato Coulis

Herb Oil

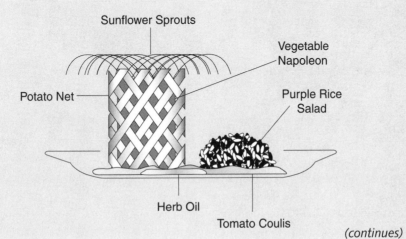

Sunflower Sprouts

Vegetable
Napoleon

Potato Net

Purple Rice
Salad

Herb Oil

Tomato Coulis

(continues)

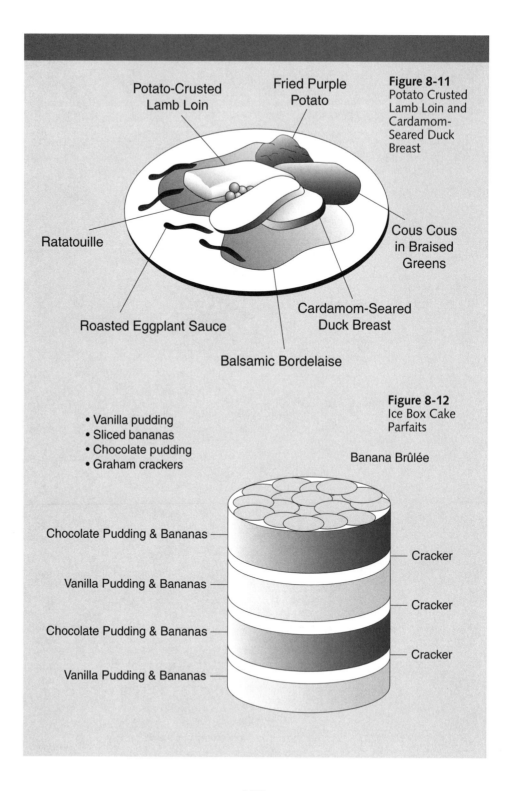

Potato-Crusted Lamb Loin

Fried Purple Potato

Figure 8-11
Potato Crusted Lamb Loin and Cardamom-Seared Duck Breast

Ratatouille

Cous Cous in Braised Greens

Roasted Eggplant Sauce

Cardamom-Seared Duck Breast

Balsamic Bordelaise

Figure 8-12
Ice Box Cake Parfaits

- Vanilla pudding
- Sliced bananas
- Chocolate pudding
- Graham crackers

Banana Brûlée

Chocolate Pudding & Bananas

Cracker

Vanilla Pudding & Bananas

Cracker

Chocolate Pudding & Bananas

Cracker

Vanilla Pudding & Bananas

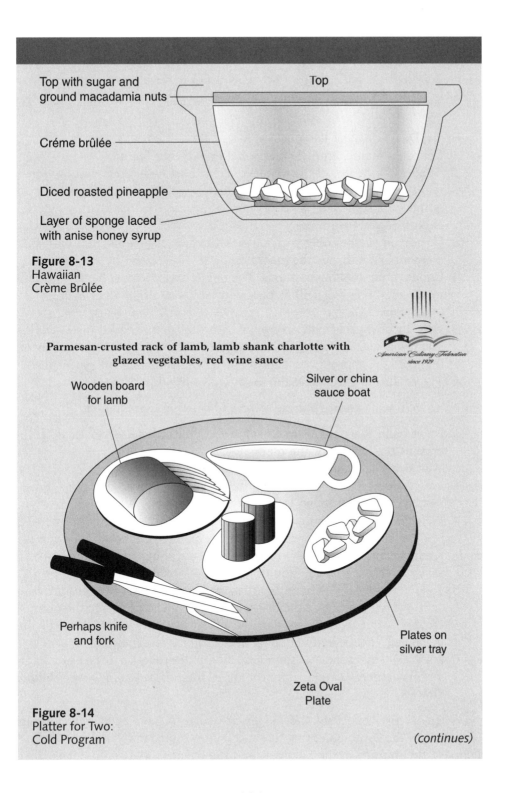

Top with sugar and
ground macadamia nuts

Top

Créme brûlée

Diced roasted pineapple

Layer of sponge laced
with anise honey syrup

Figure 8-13
Hawaiian
Crème Brûlée

**Parmesan-crusted rack of lamb, lamb shank charlotte with
glazed vegetables, red wine sauce**

Wooden board
for lamb

Silver or china
sauce boat

Perhaps knife
and fork

Plates on
silver tray

Zeta Oval
Plate

Figure 8-14
Platter for Two:
Cold Program

(continues)

101

Exercise 2: Building a Plate around a Main Item

I have found this exercise to be a proven winner in developing plates that can then be used to build solid menus. Follow these steps:

PLATE DEVELOPMENT FROM MAIN MENU ITEM

1. Choose a theme, ethnicity, seasonality, or other feature.
2. Choose the center-of-the-plate item. In most cases, this will be a protein item, but it could also be a pasta or vegetarian item as well. Step 2 is the important one, as everything from here is based on what you choose as your main item.
3. Decide on surrounding components, the accoutrements, that will complement and enhance the main item.
4. Choose your cooking methods. The objective is twofold here: you want to use methods that will display your skills and that add flavor as you build your dish.
5. Add flavoring that will give your dish that extra-special taste. Define what you want to accomplish and tie it into your theme or concept; then add, as appropriate, glazes, spices, or aromatics and garnishes.
6. The final step is to name the menu—give it a descriptive title.

Now we'll walk through these steps using actual ingredients:

1. For a main plate we want to achieve a Southwestern-American influence as the theme for the menu.
2. We select the main item to be brisket of beef.
3. We choose as our surrounding items Vidalia onions, potatoes, green beans, sourdough bread, and gravy.
4. We decide our cooking methods will be as follows: for the beef, a braise; for the onions, deep-fry; for the potatoes, mashed; and for the green beans, sauté. We will toast the sourdough bread and make a gravy from the braising liquid.
5. To add flavor to enhance this dish and create synergy with our concept, we will barbeque the brisket and add ancho chilies to the onions; cream, butter, and nutmeg to the potatoes; butter and bacon to the beans; and extra virgin olive oil and garlic on the toast.
6. Let's call this delicious-sounding menu: "Barbecued Brisket of Beef, with Whipped Potatoes, Country-Style Green Beans, and Crispy Vidalia Onions."

When tasting this dish, the judges are sure to have their expectations exceeded by the complementing flavors of ancho spice in the onions, the garlic toast, the nutmeg in the potatoes, and the bacon in the green beans.

MAKING IT TASTE GOOD: THE IMPORTANCE OF FLAVOR

I don't think I have to stress how critical it is that your dishes be flavorful—that they taste good. Taste is the main criterion for judges in the tasting room. If, as they say in show business, you leave them wanting more, you will know you have done your job. This is not to say that flavor is all, but without it, everything else in your dish will fail to impress. Moreover, achieving the right flavor for a dish or an entire menu makes every other aspect of food preparation easier, for foods that work well together flavor-wise lend themselves to easy and natural presentation.

As I said in Chapter 6, foods whose flavor profiles harmonize result in successful dishes and menus. Some complementary food harmonies you will want to consider for your hot food competition menu are:

- Rich with lean
- Spicy with bland
- Smoky with sweet
- Sweet with sour
- Sweet with spicy

You, as a chef, must recognize and take the time to learn about the six basic flavor categories, which will enable you to approach with confidence the development stage of your competition food. These six flavors are listed, along with their sensations, in Table 8-1.

Now consider this example of using the six flavor profiles with a "dish" we're all familiar with: the hamburger. It may surprise you to learn that the humble hamburger offers many flavor profiles—when cooked correctly:

- Sweet: ketchup and tomato
- Sour: pickle

TABLE 8-1 Flavors and Their Sensations

Flavor	Sensation
Sweet	Happiness, richness, moisture
Sour	Sharp, biting, sometimes unpleasant
Bitter	Biting, lingering melancholy
Spicy	Energetic, lively, sometimes unexpected
Salty	Dry, sharp, sometimes harsh
Plain	Ordinary, usual, no surprise

- Bitter: lettuce
- Spicy: spice rub for burger meat
- Salty: sea salt on tomato
- Plain: the roll

Chances are, you won't cook hamburgers for your hot food competition, but it's important to recognize that even something as simple as a hamburger can be broken down into flavor categories.

As essential to understanding the flavor categories and their connection to one another is to acknowledge the value of using seasonal foods in your competition menus. I mentioned this earlier, in the context of general development guidelines, but I want to address it here, too. Often, by using the seasons as your guide for food choices, you can to create winning dishes while using food items that are at their peak of freshness and flavor. When you think fall, for example, what comes to mind? Apples, pears, root vegetables; cinnamon, clove, all-spice, butternut squash, pumpkin, venison, and so much more. Now imagine a crispy pork shank with foie gras and apple butter over clove-spice lentils to tantalize the judges' taste buds. Creating a menu with the seasons in mind ensures that you will use products that are at their optimum in flavor, thus resulting in a spectacular finished dish.

If you study the flavor profiles of food and condiments, as well as ethnic cuisines and seasonal foods, you will have no trouble creating flavorful, tasty,

TABLE 8-2   Key Terms Used to Describe Flavor

Term	Description
Sweet	Sugary, saccharine; can be cloying if overdone
Fruity	Sweet, as in ripe; can be acidic or meaty, depending on the fruit
Floury	Gluey, starchy
Fatty	Greasy, oily, buttery
Nutty	Depending on nut, sometimes sweet, with a little "bite"; meaty, rich
Spicy	Piquant, hot, peppery, lively, depending on the spice
Pungent	Intense, sharp, sometimes sour; highly seasoned
Acidic	Sour, vinegary, tart
Salty	Piquant, earthy
Bitter	Harsh, biting, acid

TABLE 8-3 Key Terms Used to Describe Texture

Term	Description
Coarse	Rough, unprocessed, gritty
Creamy	Soft, smooth, resembling cream
Crumbly	Breakable, friable; falls apart readily into small(er) particles
Fluid	Liquid, watery
Hard	Solid, compacted, tight; firm to the touch
Smooth	Even, free from projections; silky
Tough	Resilient; chewy; sometimes fibrous, stringy, or sinewy
Watery	Soggy, saturated; fluid, liquefied
Viscous	Semifluid; resistance to flow
Flow	Quality of movement; e.g., water

TABLE 8-4 Key Terms Used to Describe Aroma

Term	Description
Aromatic	Sweet-scented, perfumed, fragrant
Fruity	Depending on the fruit, can be citrusy, sweet, or pungent
Earthy	Musty, moldy
Fishy	Scent of the sea, saltwater
Fatty	Greasy, oily, buttery
Nutty	Toasty
Burnt	Roasted, caramelized, grilled
Smoky	Scent of burning wood or plant material
Pungent	Sharp, acrid, strong, piquant, biting
Acidic	Sour, vinegary, tart, astringent, sharp
Chemical	Metallic, unnatural, unfamiliar
Foul	Unpleasant; putrid, rancid

TABLE 8-5   Key Terms Used to Describe Color/Consistency

Color or Consistency	Description
Transparent	Clear, glassy; capable of transmitting light
Translucent	See "transparent"
Opaque	Impenetrable to light, nontransparent; cloudy, filmy
Yellow	Connotes light, brightness; bounty—e.g., lemons, squash, peppers, etc.
Brown	Evokes richness, flavorful—e.g., chocolate, cinnamon, beef
Red	Evokes ripeness, richness—wine, cherries, roses, tomatoes
Green	Verdant, grassy, leafy; evocative of nature/ natural elements
White	Evokes richness, creaminess—sauces, puddings, cheeses
Black	Connotes overdone, sooty; also, richness, variety

and sensible dishes that are sure to score you big in competition—and at work every day. As you do that, keep in mind the terms listed in Tables 8-2 through 8-5 to stimulate your thoughts when thinking of how flavors, textures, aromas, color, consistency, and seasonality can impact the food you cook.

 ## ADDING THE FINAL STRATEGY: SETTING UP THE KITCHEN

Your success in the competition kitchen—that is, the ability to score high points from the kitchen judges—will be based on the following phases of production: your *game plan,* your *mise en place,* your *cooking,* your *service.* Let's go through these one by one.

Game Plan

Your game plan is all about organization. Do you know what you are going to prepare? Do you have the food items you need? Do you have the equipment (large and small) and space needed to produce the items you have selected? Have you practiced in advance so that you know you can produce and serve your items in the time allowed?

Mise en Place

Mise en place is French for "putting into place"; or, more appropriately in this context, "a place for everything and everything in its place." Have you organized the produce and dry goods you need, and in the correct amounts, to produce the menu? Have you set up your workspace so as to prevent cross-contamination in accordance with proper sanitation practices?

Is the oven turned on to the required temperature? Have you set the cutting board on a wet paper towel to prevent it from sliding? Are all perishable items stored properly in the refrigerator? Are refrigerated items arranged for easy access? Have you left space to store prepped items?

What about your pots and pans? Have you selected the proper pan and size for the job intended? Have you set aside serving pans to hold the finished product?

Cooking

Cooking is a four-stage process:

1. Prepreparation: Slicing, dicing; trussing, seasoning.
2. Preparation: Start with items having the longest cooking times.
3. Clean: As you go.
4. Finishing: Your objective is to complete items as close to service time as possible.

Service

Service is a two-part procedure: *Setup* and *actual service*. For your service setup line you'll need:

- Hot plates, serving spoons, forks, ingredients, garnish, etc.
- Wiping cloth for plate rim
- Heat lamps, chafers
- Tablecloth
- Finishing tray with oils, syrups, etc.

For actual service, you'll need:

- Plates, neat and clean; food hot
- Food arranged properly and consistently on all plates
- Presentation in a timely manner

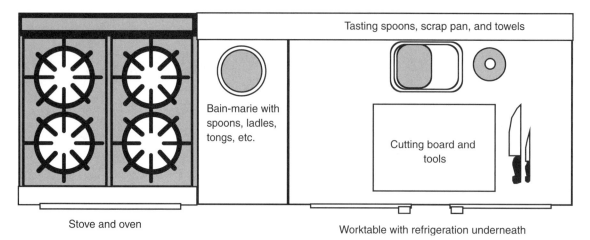

Tasting spoons, scrap pan, and towels

Bain-marie with spoons, ladles, tongs, etc.

Cutting board and tools

Stove and oven

Worktable with refrigeration underneath

Figure 8-15
Station Setup
for Hot Food
Competition

To help you visualize these important concepts, look at Figure 8-15, which shows an ideal station setup for a hot food competition.

 **CONCLUSION**

Your overall strategy for success in the culinary competition is to be in control, yet make it look natural—to show you are confident and organized. The image you want to portray is one of confidence, that of a true professional who cares about what you do and can demonstrate that care with craftsman-like actions.

CHAPTER
9

Taking the Mystery Basket Challenge

I've mentioned the Mystery Basket competition on several occasions previously; I've even alluded to it as one of the greatest challenges a cook or chef can face in the hot food kitchen. In this chapter, I will detail the components of this competition, which is designed to test culinarians of all skill levels.

Why is the Mystery Basket considered by many the "test of tests" in the culinary competition arena? The short answer is because it is the great unknown. The clock tick, tick, ticks, and you must find a way to achieve those two golden elements—simplicity and elegance—in your meal without the usual preplanning process, without the conceptual development stage,

TAKE THE CHALLENGE
Since the introduction of contemporary competitions, the number of Mystery Basket competitions has dropped, which I think is a shame. It seems more chefs today prefer the less stressful events, at which they show up with a menu and have an hour to cook two courses. In contrast, the Mystery Basket is the challenge of a lifetime—a chef's lifetime. Just making the attempt, is an education like no other. Every Mystery Basket you attempt makes you a better cook, which is reason enough to attempt this challenge.

SOME THINGS REMAIN THE SAME

Though the Mystery Basket is a competition unlike any other, the preparatory guidelines remain the same as for all culinary competition: (1) Read the application thoroughly. (2) Thoroughly fill out the application as directed previously in this book. (3) Review the national rules and guidelines. (4) Develop an action plan beginning with the application process and carrying through to the competition.

and without a review process. It is a challenge that gets the blood moving through your veins and brings out the best in the best of cooks.

PREPARING FOR THE UNKNOWN

The intention of the Mystery Basket competition is to test your ability to cook "on the fly," with the ingredients presented to you. So the question is, how do you prepare and practice for the unknown?

A practice method I used prior to my Master's Chef exam was to invite some close friends over, with the instruction that they bring enough food for a four-course meal—no restrictions, whatever they wanted. Not only did I learn a lot, it was fun and gave me some fond memories. An even more challenging version is to ask your friends to invite company to their place, so that you have to cook what they buy and in their kitchen.

Sound interesting? Now let me give you the nuts and bolts—or should I say the meat and potatoes—of this most compelling of culinary competitions.

HOW THE MYSTERY BASKET WORKS

The ingredients for the Mystery Basket, which are never revealed in advance, vary for each competition, but they are always the same for all competitors in the competition at hand. For an individual competition, there will be enough food for 3 or 4 courses and 10 portions per course.

Each basket will include no fewer than three, and no more than five, main items—main items being meat, fish, poultry, or game. Contestants must utilize *all* main items to some degree in their menus; there should be no reason to return anything. Again, the weight of the main items must be sufficient to prepare a 3- or 4-course meal of 10 portions each. Note, however, if one of the main items is oysters or clams, or another "quantity" item, a count, rather than weight, should be used.

The 10 portions are used as follows:

- Two are for the judges to taste.
- One is for the judges' critique and, later, the archival photo display.
- One is for media photos.

■ Six are served for lunch. Depending on the show, the host may sell tickets to guests or attendees, or the tickets may be handed out to VIPs, sponsors, and so on.

In addition to the main items, there will be items to produce a salad, if the lettuce is not included in the kitchen staples, as well as two or three vegetable items and one or two starch items, again, if a starch is not present in the kitchen staples.

TIP
Using whole items with bone is encouraged to show the fundamental skills of the competitors.

Procedure

Prior to the competition, during the judges' meeting, competitors draw for starting sequence and kitchen assignments. Kitchen assignments follow the starting sequence—that is, the competitor who starts first is given kitchen number 1 and so forth. At 20-minute intervals, each competitor receives the Mystery Basket containing the selection of ingredients. While competitors are waiting to begin, they are kept away from the kitchen area so as not to gain an unfair advantage by seeing the contents of the basket.

MAKEUP OF JUDGING PANEL
The judges' panel must consist of a minimum of four to five American Culinary Federation (ACF) approved judges, one or two for kitchen proctors and three for a blind tasting.

No later than 30 minutes after receiving the basket, each competitor must submit his or her menu to one of the competition proctors. No substitutions for items in the basket can be made and, as noted above, all competitors must use all items in the basket to some degree. After submitting his or her recipe, each competitor is allotted four hours cooking time. Serving begins (the serving window opens) when the first competitor reaches the four-hour limit. Each competitor is allotted a 20-minute window in which to serve all of his or her courses. If a competitor misses his or her turn, he or she will be disqualified.

The Facilities

Mystery Basket contestants share storeroom and kitchen facilities.

COMMUNITY STOREROOM

The community storeroom, from which all contestants may draw supplies, will generally include, though not be limited to, the items listed in Figure 9-1. As for the kitchen equipment list, all competitors must receive, at least two weeks prior to the competition, a complete list of items available in the community storeroom. In no case should items in the Mystery Basket duplicate items available in the community storeroom.

Figure 9-1
A Sample
Community
Storeroom List

Produce	Fresh Herbs	Groceries
Carrots	Basil	Dijon mustard
Celery	Chives	Gelatin, powder and sheets
Garlic	Dill	Olive oil
White onions	Mint	Sugar
Red onions	Parsley	Soy sauce
Idaho potatoes	Rosemary	Tabasco
Shallots	Tarragon	Teriyaki sauce
Leeks	Thyme	Tomato paste
Fruits	**Dairy**	Vegetable oil
Lemons	Butter	Worcestershire sauce
Limes	Cream	Hazelnuts
Oranges	Eggs	Pecans
Staples	Milk	Vanilla beans
All-purpose flour	Cream cheese	Plain rice
Whole wheat flour	Sour cream	**Stocks**
Bread crumbs	Yogurt	Chicken stock
White bread	Ricotta	Fish stock
Pastry flour	Crème fraiche	Veal stock
Cornstarch		**Spice Rack**: as available in kitchen

STUDENT ASSISTANTS/APPRENTICES

Student assistants are made available to Mystery Basket competitors to help with basic prepwork, for example, the ricing of potatoes or cleaning of lettuce greens. They will always be assigned by a blind drawing on the day of the competition.

To qualify as an assistant, the person must be registered in a bona fide culinary program; preferably, he or she will be registered in an American Culinary Federation Educational Institute (ACFEI) apprenticeship program or enrolled as a student in a culinary program accredited by the ACFEI Accrediting Commission. Student assistants must always be assigned by a blind drawing.

In addition, student assistants must have a solid understanding of basic cooking fundamentals (e.g., blanching of vegetables, preparing a sachet d'epices or bouquet garni) and terminology and be able to follow instructions regarding weights, measures, and equipment needs. These students must also have mastered the basic knife skills—mincing, chopping, and dicing—and be able to differentiate between julienne, brunoise, batonnet, chiffonade, tourné. To that end, students who apply to assist Mystery Basket competitors will be screened in these areas.

This is a win-win arrangement: the Mystery Basket competitor gains a much-needed helping hand during a high-pressure contest, and the assistant has the opportunity to gain knowledge and experience.

THE COMMUNITY KITCHEN

The community kitchen should include small appliances, such as meat slicers, pasta machines, and blenders, to be shared by all competitors. At least two weeks prior to the competition, all competitors will receive a complete listing of the specific items available to them in the community kitchen. Contestants are allowed to bring only their tools (i.e., knives and cutters) although organizers may specify any other (and the number of) small appliances that competitors will be permitted to bring in.

In addition to the community kitchen facilities and equipment, each Mystery Basket contestant must be provided with a workstation that consists of:

- Worktable space, with at least two 6- to 8-feet tables
- Cutting board
- Four- to six-burner stove with oven

However, two competitors may share the following:

- Large double-door refrigerator
- Double sinks with running water
- Double-stack conventional oven or combination oven

KITCHEN CORRECTNESS

In all Mystery Basket competition facilities, a safe and efficient working environment must be maintained, and adequate equipment must be provided to enable competitors to do their job.

ATTACKING THE BASKET

I recommend you approach the basket methodically, as follows:

1. Separate the main proteins and main salad greens. Place them all on a separate trays.
2. Review the remaining items. The menu should become obvious to you, if you have done as advised in this book and studied the flavor profiles and mastered the fundamentals.

Let's assume the basket contains a pork loin or pork butt and Savoy cabbage, apples, root vegetables, cider, and a loaf of bread. What comes to my mind immediately is this menu:

Braised Pork with Apple Stuffing

Cider-Braised Cabbage with Glazed Root Vegetables

If, instead, the basket contains shrimp, two whole snappers, and clams, and the accoutrement items are fennel, plum tomatoes, and salsify, then what comes to mind is the following:

MENU TITLE

Roasted Snapper and Shrimp over
a Stew of Tomatoes, Salsify and Fennel

Don't forget: You have only 30 minutes to write your menu. Therefore, plan to prepare food you are comfortable cooking, and execute tried-and-true dishes you are familiar with. As I've said before, if you have never made a hot terrine, the competition arena is not the place to cook your first one. As you write your menu, focus on great flavor combinations first and foremost; in most cases, all other items will follow naturally from that.

Another important element to remember as you write your menu is to plan to execute a variety of cooking fundamentals, to show your diverse skill set, which together produce great food. Consider what might serve as a unique or stand-out item: for example, add to a great-tasting soup some contrived garnishes, then plan to pour the soup at the table. The 1988 ACF culinary team did just that: they developed a stuffed pasta that looked like an asparagus to add to the soup.

Keep the menu practical and sensible. I've said this over and over, but it's that important. You don't want to see the judges shaking their heads or asking too many questions among each other. Another important piece of advice is not to assume that something you prepare at your workplace will be appropriate in competition. Customers generally are not acutely aware of cooking fundamentals and good flavor profiles; the judges are.

TIP

If you can write your menu in 15 minutes, you will have an extra 15 minutes to get started. Write it in 10 minutes, you gain 20 minutes. But don't write so fast that you sacrifice sense, thereby putting yourself in a bind after you begin cooking.

And You're Off

"Come out of the gate" strong—that's my advice. Don't try to pace yourself then make a big push at the end, as this can only lead to sloppiness and mistakes. Pay attention to details that make a difference and impress judges: have plate wipes made and ready; have service tools, heat lamps, and oven temperatures set to go; cover sauces; lay a tablecloth on your service area.

Respect the product, *always*—if there is a turkey in your mystery basket, make sure the dish will taste like turkey, that the sauce yells out turkey! For example, roasting the breast on the rack properly and then taking the thigh or leg meat and producing a ballotine combined with the proper vegetables, starch, and flavoring profiles will garner you big points. In contrast, taking the breast and pounding it, stuffing it, and serving it with a red wine sauce will not. Again: Understand your food and flavor combinations—turkey and sage, lobster and vanilla, pork and anise, fish and citrus, and so on.

Finally, work clean and make your movements in the kitchen seamless. And don't forget to smile; you should be having fun doing what you love.

Exercise: Mystery Basket Number One

Figure 9-2 lists the contents of a sample mystery basket. Before you read ahead to the menu I've devised from these ingredients, try to come up with one on your own. Here are some hints: I first wrote down the proteins, then matched them to items that would complement them and give a tasty flavor profile. And, note, I view the salad as a palate cleanser to prepare for the next course. Now, here's the menu:

Quantity	Description
1 ea	Leg of lamb
4 lbs	Grouper, whole
2 lbs	Bay scallops
2 lbs	Yukon gold potatoes
1 lb	Green beans
3 ea	Eggplant
5 ea	Lola Rosa lettuce
10 ea	Broccoli rabe
8 oz	Walnuts
4 ea	Apples (Golden Delicious)
1 ea	Jicama
4 hds	Radicchio
1 root	Ginger, fresh
4 ea	Plantains
3 ea	Yellow bell peppers

Figure 9-2
Market Basket
Number One

MENU TITLE

First Plate: Pan-Roasted Grouper, Plantain-Wrapped Bay Scallops, and Spiced Ginger Green Beans

Salad Course: Salad of Radicchio and Lola Rosa Lettuce with Jicama and Apple Straws, Honey Walnuts, and Goat Cheese Dressing

Main Plate: Roast Leg of Lamb (Deboned, seasoned and made into a little roast); Eggplant and Yellow Pepper Relish, Broccoli Rabe; Garlic Mashed Potatoes with Rosemary Lamb Gravy

Pastry Optional: N/A

Why not test yourself by practicing this menu in the time allotted? Then challenge yourself further with the basket ingredients given in Figures 9-3 and 9-4. Set that timer!

 ## CONCLUSION: COMPETITION REVIEW SESSION

In conclusion here, I recommend that as part of the exercises above, you take the time to review these elements common to all competitions:

Quantity	Description
2 lbs	Swordfish
1½ lbs	Shrimp, whole body intact
4 lbs	Center cut pork with trimmings
1 lb	Orzo
1 lb	Quinoa
4 ea	Artichokes
1 lb	Snap peas, or Chinese long beans
2 ea	Star fruit
1½ lbs	Assorted dried fruits
6 ea	Bosc pears
8 oz	Baby greens
2 ea	Belgium endive
1 bunch	Kale
2 bunch	Arugula
1 bulb	Celeriac

Figure 9-3
Market Basket
Number Two

NOTE
In Mystery Basket competitions, china will be provided for you. You will need to check if you want to bring your own.

TIP
When choosing china, be aware of current style trends, such as using mixed china, a variety of shapes, and little containers.

Presentation

Presentation, as you know by now, is the final "ingredient" in your menu preparation. Proper presentation makes delicious food taste even better. Remember to have at the ready:

Acceptable containers for hot food

Copper dishes

Stainless-steel platters

Earthenware dishes

China dinner plates

Polished pewter

Silver platters for service

Pyrex

You'll also need to consider the following components when choosing china:

Design
☐ Shape of china
☐ Depth of eating surface to rim

Color
☐ Generally light and neutral; white is best. (Stay away from too much color or pattern unless it reflects your food concept.)
☐ Must complement the food.

Size
☐ Compatible with portion size
☐ Capable of being used with a variety of courses

Practicality
☐ Delicacy of china, especially the rim
☐ Size of rim and eating surface

Creativity

I've cautioned you about balancing creativity with sensibility, and for good reason: it's a delicate balancing act to be both creative and sensible in culinary competitions. The following list will give you clues as to what comprises judging criteria as far as creativity is concerned:

- New food combination
- New shapes
- New layout ideas
- New garnishes (functional)
- Rework or modernization of traditional techniques and presentation
- A contemporary spin on a classical dish

Workmanship/Craftsmanship

Here I want to detail the criteria judges use to rate skill level in the fundamentals.

PROPER HANDLING OF INGREDIENTS
- Cleaning (e.g., squid eyes, shrimp veins)
- Peeling (e.g., avocados, tomatoes, kiwi, etc.)
- Scaling fish
- Trimming meat (proper butchering, deboning, correct thickness of fat layer, etc.)
- Proper preparation of forcemeats (e.g., smooth texture; moisture; good color)
- Use of the proper method of butchery, followed by cooking that matches the cuts

KNIFE SKILLS
- Carving (complete, even slices; clean edges)
- Slicing—bias, bevel, straight, wedge (thin is more desirable than thick)
- Shaping (e.g, tourné, basic knife cuts, etc.)

GARNISH ASSEMBLY
- Inlays, if attempted, must be exact. (If an inlay is even slightly "off," the highly structured configuration of this type of garnish will be magnified. Generally, a random garnish is preferred over an exact inlay garnish,

Quantity	Description
2 ea	Rabbits, skinned and peeled
3 ea	Rainbow trout, whole
3 dz	Black farm-raised mussels, whole
1 hds	Savoy cabbage
1 bunch	Salsify
4 ea	Turnips
5 ea	Anjou pears
1 bx	Phyllo dough
1/2 pt	Sour cream
3 ea	Granny Smith apples
2 oz	Poppy seeds
2 bulbs	Fennel
2 hds	Frisée
1 bunch	Cilantro
1 bunch	Collard greens
1 lb	Cornmeal

Figure 9-4
Market Basket
Number Three

particularly in hot food.) Contrived garnishes must be exact and prepared with the correct process.

- Garnishes must make sense to the food they are paired with.

Hot Food Assembly

- Hot terrines (no air pockets; size; position of inlay, if any)
    - Hot galantines and ballotines (size; meeting of skin; color of skin after cooking)
    - Hot mousseline (consistency; smoothness of forcemeat)
    - Tarts and pies (thickness of crust)

Proper Cooking Techniques

- Braising: not stringy when sliced
- Poaching: moist, not overcooked
- Roasting: proper color—pink, not bloody
- Smoking: rich color, proper cure
- Sautéing: evenly browned, moist
- Steaming: proper color
- Baking: proper crust thickness and color
- Deep-fat frying: no greasiness

> **VARIETY IS THE SPICE OF COOKING**
> By using a variety of cooking techniques, you will automatically add different textures to your food, such as roasted whole meat with poached sausage, baked crust with braised meats, or deep-fried fish with boiled vegetable.

Color

- Aim for measured color variety—avoid a circus effect (e.g., pastel colors with one strong color).
- Choose foods that taste good together and have a natural synergy because of flavor profiles; they will naturally harmonize in color.
- The color should highlight the cooking techniques used.
- To avoid homogeneous colors that appear artificial, even when obtained from natural means, add visual texture (e.g., chopped herbs to a smooth green forcemeat; or saffron threads to a smooth yellow-fish mousseline).
- Textured colors, mentioned above, tend to be more appetizing than pure colors.

Nutritional Balance

- Your food should display an understanding of current nutritional balance.

APPENDIX 9-1 SAMPLE SCORE SHEETS

Figure 9-5 shows a sample of the score sheets judges use to rank entrants in the Mystery Basket competition.

Hot Food Score Sheet/Blind Tasting

Service/Tasting Judges

Competitor:_____ Judge:_____

Show:_____ Date:_____

Criteria	Max. pts	1st	2nd	3rd	4th	
Serving methods and presentation	5 pts.					
Portion size	5 pts.					
Nutritional balance	10 pts.					
Menu and ingredient compatibility	5 pts.					
Creativity	10 pts.					
Flavor/taste, texture, doneness	30 pts.					
Individual course scores	65 pts					

Award Guidelines	
40 pts.:	Gold Medal with Honors
36–39 pts.:	Gold Medal
32–35 pts.:	Silver Medal
28–31 pts.:	Bronze Medal
24–27 pts.:	Culinary Diploma

Subtotal_____

÷ number of courses_____

Service and Tasting Score_____

Menu and Descriptions and Comments

1st Course:

2nd Course:

3rd Course:

4th Course:

Additional Comments:

Figure 9-5
Sample Hot Food Score Sheets

(continues)

119

Hot Food Score Sheet/Blind Tasting

Kitchen/Floor Judges

Competitor:_____ Judge:_____

Show:_____ Date:_____

Criteria	Max. pts	
Mise en place/Organization	5 pts.	
Sanitation procedures/cleanliness	5 pts.	
Apprentice coordination and task delegation	5 pts.	
Proper utilization of ingredients and leftovers	5 pts.	
Timing of service and follow-up	5 pts.	
Cooking techniques, skills, and fundamentals	10 pts.	
Individual course scores	35 pts.	

Award Guidelines
40 pts.: Gold Medal with Honors
36–39 pts.: Gold Medal
32–35 pts.: Silver Medal
28–31 pts.: Bronze Medal
24–27 pts.: Culinary Diploma

Kitchen Floor Score_____

Notes and Comments

Figure 9-5
Sample Hot Food Score Sheets

Hot Food Score Sheet/Blind Tasting

Summary Score Sheet

Competitor:_____

Show:_____ Date:_____

Kitchen/Floor Scores

Judge 1	0–35 pts.	
Judge 2	0–35 pts.	
Judge 3	0–35 pts.	
Judge 4	0–35 pts.	
Judge 5	0–35 pts.	
	Subtotal	

÷ number of judges_____

Final Kitchen Score_____

(0–35 pts)

Service/Tasting Scores

Judge 1	0–65 pts.	
Judge 2	0–65 pts.	
Judge 3	0–65 pts.	
Judge 4	0–65 pts.	
Judge 5	0–65 pts.	
	Subtotal	

÷ number of judges_____

Final Service/Tasting Score_____

(0–65 pts)

Kitchen/ Floor Score_____

+

Service/Tasting Score_____

= _____ Subtotal

(0–100 pts)

÷ 2.5 = _____ Final Score

(0–40 pts)

Award Guidelines	
40 pts.:	Gold Medal with Honors
36–39 pts.:	Gold Medal
32–35 pts.:	Silver Medal
28–31 pts.:	Bronze Medal
24–27 pts.:	Culinary Diploma

Award/Medal_____

Figure 9-5
Sample Hot Food Score Sheets

121

Judging and Scoring

t hardly needs to be said that judges play an integral role at all competitions, for they are the individuals who observe, study, review, taste, and score your cold food display or hot food entrée. Judges also set the tone for the event; they ensure that a high standard is maintained and that competition guidelines and requirements are met. Therefore, the American Culinary Federation makes every effort to ensure that those who judge fully understand its standards and guidelines. And to maintain as much as possible an atmosphere of objectivity and fairness, the ACF holds seminars for judges, not only to instruct them in the details of the evaluation process, but to ensure that they know they are expected to leave their personal opinions out of their evaluations. Thus, say, if a judge does not care for cilantro, he or she cannot penalize you if your dish includes cilantro, and you used it properly, so that it adds the right flavor to the dish and harmonizes with the food.

Nevertheless, judges, like all people, are subject to the same frailties of intent, and just saying or agreeing to be objective in a culinary competition doesn't mean they can be—it is difficult for anyone to leave their preferences and prejudices at the door. That means the judging process can be frustrating for competitors if they feel judges are unfair and give them a rating based on their own personal food preferences. That is why ACF competitions have strict guidelines for the number of judges and their credentials. Requiring three or more judges provides balanced evaluations and eliminates as much as possible any bias. The ACF also makes it the responsibility of the competition host to vet judges. In particular, if the competition has a large monetary award attached or is a major-profile event, the host must find judges who have experience in competitions, are knowledgeable about modern trends, and currently are working in a kitchen setting. The ACF judging program is reviewed here so that you, as a competitor, will know what you can expect from a judge: what a judge's responsibilities are, and the level of professionalism each must have to participate in culinary competitions. More important, this information will give you a good idea of what to expect from the judging experience. To that end, the chapter contains a number of forms that clarify the process. And because it is essential to both give and receive feedback, included is a form that competitors can fill out and send to the ACF, to voice their impressions in regard to a competition and the judges.

 ## BECOMING A JUDGE

Let me start by saying that the decision to become a judge should not be made to boost one's ego or to give greater prestige to a résumé. Rather, it is a serious responsibility: judges assess and evaluate the work of colleagues; as such, they wield great power. Depending on the quality of their feedback—critique—judges can leave a young competitor encouraged to become more committed to the profession and determined to improve; or they can discourage that same competitor to the point of disenchantment. Thus, ACF's judge approval process is one designed to make the industry confident that its judges are of the highest quality, in knowledge, experience, and integrity. Appointment as an ACF-approved culinary judge confirms that the individual has attained the highest level of trust, professionalism, respect, and ethical stature from his or her peers.

Culinary judges are expected to keep up with modern trends of competitions; they must commit to educating themselves on an ongoing basis, as opposed to relying on past accomplishments and experiences. They must, as well, familiarize themselves with a variety of cuisines, and understand the culture of ethnic foods. It is also considered their duty to be firm but fair, to demonstrate knowledge without intimidating, and remain humble regardless of their accomplishments. Anything less does a great injustice to the system and to the competitors.

A judge must also be comfortable saying, "I am not sure; let me find out for you or ask another judge who may be more knowledgeable in this area." No one can be an expert in all areas of cuisine, and the value of being able to say "I don't know" cannot be overestimated.

WHAT JUDGES JUDGE

There are two types of judges—floor judges and tasting judges—and they evaluate different aspects of the culinary competition.

Floor Judges

The primary purview of the floor judge is organization. As they judge, they are, essentially, asking these questions:

- Is the workspace kept clear of nonessentials—for example, a mixer that is not needed for the next 30 minutes? Is the workspace cluttered or organized? Is the setup of the workspace sensible?

- Does the contestant work systematically, on one job at a time?

- Is food being handled properly, following current guidelines as to temperature and safety?

- Is the correct knife for the job utilized; and are proper cutting motions evident? Are knives kept sharp?

- Are products stored properly and at the right temperature? Are the refrigerator, rack cart, knife, and equipment storage well organized?

- Is useable waste stored properly for future use?

- Is the table free from debris? Are floor spills attended to quickly? Is the dish area being used as a "storage dump?" Are cutting boards kept scrupulously clean? Are areas kept sanitized, particularly during fish to meat to vegetable or dairy transitions? Is the toolbox/knife bag clean and sanitary inside?

- Is the sanitizing solution at the right strength, and is it being used properly? Are towels used correctly? Or, for example, is a towel used to wipe debris off a table and then to wipe a knife or a plate? Is the apron being used as a hand wipe? Are gloves used for the last contact with food—for example, plating up.

- Are smooth transitions made from one job to another? Is there a logical progression of jobs—for example, to avoid chopping herbs or mincing garlic on several occasions? Is proper timing of menu items, cooking techniques, and skills in evidence? *(continues)*

125

WHAT JUDGES JUDGE *(continued)*

- Are classical cooking techniques followed? How many different techniques have been displayed? Is the technique cited in the recipe adhered to? For example, is mirepoix browned properly, not just heated? Is the product roasted correctly and basted as needed, not just placed in the oven?

- Are butchery and boning skills efficient? Is there "profitable" removal of muscle or fish from a bone? Are sinew and/or fat removal and correct tying methods displayed?

- Are menu items held the proper amount of time? Do meats have the time to rest? Is serving done within the five-minute window?

- Does the contestant make an organized withdrawal from the kitchen, leaving it as clean as he or she found it?

Tasting Judges

Tasting judges evaluate serving methods and presentation, as well as taste. They address questions such as:

- Is hot food hot and cold food cold (including plates)? Is food fresh and colorful, visibly seasoned, presented with some height, easy to eat, and pleasing to the eye?

- Does food have great aroma, to stimulate the appetite?

- Are meat/fish slices even, shingled correctly, and sliced in a way that makes sense for hot food? Are items placed closely together to help maintain temperature, or separated in a pleasing way?

- Is proper portion size and nutritional balance evident? Are the components of the meal balanced so that the main item is complemented in size/amount by the accompanying garnish(es) and/or sauce?

- Are nutritional standards adhered to in relation to the dish? That is, is the protein weight within reasonable amounts such as 4-6 ounces for lunch and 8-12 ounces for dinner, for all courses?

- Is there ingredient compatibility? Do ingredient colors harmonize naturally because of flavor combinations? Do ingredients and flavor components harmonize perfectly?

- Has the contestant demonstrated creativity and practicality? For example, could the dish be produced just as easily for a party of a 100 as behind the cook's line on a busy night? Does the dish show a degree of difficulty, using skills and creative flair, as opposed to something copied and overused? Or, if using an old or classical idea, has a new, contemporary concept been employed to transform the dish?

WHAT JUDGES JUDGE *(continued)*

- Does the dish have the correct flavor, taste, texture, and doneness? Has the contestant shown respect for the food—for example, the duck broth tastes like duck and the Dover sole is not covered with Creole sauce.

- Are doneness temperatures correct? Are stated vegetable cuts correct? Have the stated cooking techniques been applied correctly? Do the textures correspond to what was implied in the recipe? Does the flavor of the sauce or vinaigrette reflect what the recipe stated, and is it of the correct consistency? Does it taste great?

- Does the menu have a thread or a theme running throughout—for example, is it a regional, ethnic, seasonal, or celebration menu? Are all courses in sync with the menu; or, for example, has an Asian-type dish been inserted into an American-type menu? Are there any erratic or overdominant flavors that disrupt the flow of the theme?

- Do the dishes portray a high level of skill and exactness? Does the number of different skills employed throughout the menu distinguish the caliber of the cook?

Selection Procedure

To become a culinary judge, one must have proven him- or herself in competition and demonstrated good judgment. Only with this background can he or she be placed in a position to evaluate others in culinary competitions. The screening procedure and selection process for culinary judges must, therefore, ensure that only individuals with impeccable qualifications are selected.

To that end, the ACF-approved culinary judge program was established to provide a nationwide pool of qualified judges for culinary competitions. Definitive prerequisites for approval were established, along with criteria to ensure that qualifications remain current. (Because the culinary profession is constantly updating its trends and standards, a system had to be put in place to guarantee that those who judge remain up to date.)

After satisfying a number of prerequisites (listed below) and filling out an application (see Figure 10-1), candidate judges are required to apprentice at a minimum of five ACF-approved culinary competitions under the supervision of approved judges and attend a training seminar at a regional conference or national convention (the candidate is solely responsible for coordinating his or her assignment as a judge with the senior competition judge and for attendance funding requirements).

To: Chairman, ACF Culinary Competition Committee (CCC):

I hereby apply for approval as an ACF-approved culinary judge. I understand it is my responsibility to complete all prerequisites as outlined in the ACF-approved *Culinary Competition Manual*. I further understand that upon completion of all prerequisites my qualifications for judging will be reviewed by the CCC, and their determination as to my approval or requirement for additional training will be final.

Date of Application: _____

Name: _____

Address: _____

City/State/Zip: _____

Phone Numbers

Work: _____

Home: _____

Fax: _____

E-mail: _____

ACF Certifications/Expiration Dates:

_____/_____

_____/_____

_____/_____

ACF Membership # _____

Date of Birth _____

Employment Establishment:

_____

Position: _____

Address: _____

City/State/Zip:

_____

Competition Experience: ACF and WACS (attach continuation sheet if required)

Medal	Type	Competition Date
_____	_____	_____
_____	_____	_____
_____	_____	_____
_____	_____	_____
_____	_____	_____

Candidate's Signature: _____

Approved for Judge in Training: _____

(CCC Chair)

Date: _____

Figure 10-1
Application for ACF-Approved Culinary Judge

Following completion of these training requirements, candidates are reviewed by the Culinary Competition Committee (CCC) and either approved or recommended for additional training. Decisions of the committee are considered final. Administration of the judge program is performed by the Events Management Department, while the authority for approving judges is reserved for the CCC. Prerequisites for judges are as follows:

- Be an ACF member in good standing.
- Be ACF-certified at the Certified Sous Chef (CSC)/Certified Working Pastry Chef (CWPC) level or higher.
- Have won a minimum of three gold medals (one in category F, one in categories A, B, or C, and one in either category K or P). (These categories are defined later in the chapter and in Chapter 13.)
- These medals must be from the ACF, the World Association of Cooks Society (WACS), or the Hotel Olympia (where every two years a culinary exhibit features some of the top talent in the United Kingdom). Judges are also encouraged to compete internationally, to gain valuable experience.
- Be approved for judge training by the chair of the Culinary Competition Committee.

IN LIEU OF MEDALS
Achieving Certified Master Chef status will fulfill medal requirements.

Experience criteria for judges is as follows:

- Serve as an apprentice judge for a minimum of five ACF-approved culinary competitions over a period of two years. Of these competitions, three must be Category F, K, or P/1-2.
- Attend a judging seminar held at a regional conference or national convention.
- Maintain ACF-approved judge qualification, which means retaining currency as an ACF member in good standing; retaining currency at the required level of ACF certification; and judging a minimum of two competitions over the past two years.

As noted, once candidates have had their applications approved, they must "judge" a minimum of five culinary competitions over the next two years under the supervision of an approved judge. During these competitions, the lead judge will evaluate the apprentice judge in the areas of culinary knowledge, professionalism, judgment, and communication skills.

Senior judges are required to complete the critique shown in Figure 10-2 on apprentice judges performing under their tenure and forward this form to the Events Management Department for filing in permanent records. The form should be mailed no later than one week following the competition. (Apprentice judges are encouraged to follow up to ensure the Events Management Department has received this documentation.) Lead judges

Senior Judge Name: _____

Competition Name: _____

Dates: _____

Sponsoring Chapter: _____

Apprentice Judge Name: _____

Please provide comments and your evaluation of the above judge candidate. All comments will be held in confidence and released only to members of the CCC if required in the performance of their duties. (Attach additional sheets, if required.)

Categories Judged (Circle) A B C D E F G H K P S

Comments on candidate in regard to the following competencies:

Culinary Knowledge Level:

Professionalism:

Judgment:

Communication Skills:

Would you recommend this candidate for approval as an ACF culinary judge? Yes _____   No _____

Comments/Recommendations:

Signature: _____

Date: _____

Figure 10-2
Apprentice Judge Critique

are expected to debrief apprentice judges following a competition, but the contents of the written critique are considered privileged information, available only to members of the CCC.

Upon completion of the five apprentice periods, applicants must notify the Events Management Department that they wish to have their records reviewed by the CCC for approval. The Events Management Department will coordinate this review for the next sequential meeting (normally, held biannually) of the CCC. Following the CCC meeting, the chair will notify the candidates of the results of the review, in writing within 30 days.

If additional action is necessary before qualification, this will be specifically outlined. Decisions of the CCC in matters related to judge candidates are considered final. Once a judge is ACF-approved, as noted above, he or she is required to maintain currency. Judge records will be reviewed annually by the Events Management Department. Notification letters will be sent to judges whose qualifications have lapsed, explaining the area(s) in question and requesting corrective action. If action is not taken, a recommendation that they be removed from the judges' list will be sent to the chair of the CCC for approval. Individuals will be subsequently notified in writing if they have been removed from the list. Again, decisions of the CCC chair are final. Acceptance by an individual as an ACF-approved judge confirms acceptance of these guidelines and the decisions of the CCC chair.

Other Forms of Procedure

Judges are required to commit to participate in competitions up to six months in advance (see Figure 10-3). Scheduling this far in advance is not always easy for judges, but it is necessary for show planners, who must budget travel expenses, print programs, and coordinate a multitude of other show elements. Judges are expected to make every effort to keep these commitments, and if they can't, they are responsible for finding a suitable replacement.

The critique shown in Figure 10-4 enables any competitor or coach (in the case of a team competition) to provide constructive remarks regarding a competition event. It is not a forum to dispute the scoring of an individual or a team; rather, it is designed to provide valuable feedback on the performance of the judging team and will be helpful for future adjustments by the Culinary Competition Committee. Therefore, remarks should be balanced in relation to the current guidelines and, with thoughtfulness, provide a remedial suggestion to the issue you are raising. Your comments should be addressed to the ACF Event Management Department, 180 Center Place Way, St. Augustine, FL 32095.

Chapter Name: _____

Chapter Address: _____

City: _____ State: _____ Zip: _____

Date: _____

Dear Chapter President/Show Chair:

By this notice, I hereby confirm that I will be available to judge your culinary competition at _____ on

_____.

Should an unforeseen circumstance preclude my participation, I will do my best to notify the lead judge immediately, and I *will coordinate* the assignment of a qualified replacement.

Sincerely,

Judge's Signature: _____ Date: _____

Name: _____

Address: _____

Phone: _____ Fax: _____

E-mail: _____

Figure 10-3
Judge's Letter of Commitment

Your Name _____

Address _____

City _____ State _____ Zip _____

Name of Show _____

ACF Chapter _____

Date of Event _____

Culinary Show Host _____

Category _____

Judging Team:

Lead Judge_____ Judge 2_____

Judge 3 _____ Judge 4 _____

(Please circle the floor judge)

Event Facility:

Were all facilities described in the competition manual provided? Was the facility available early enough for you to set up before entering the competition area? Yes_____ No _____

Floor Judge:

Were you checked in, and your ingredients inspected? Yes _____ No _____

Did the floor judge explain to you the location of your cooking area, the time to move in, and the start and finish times for your competition slot? Yes _____ No _____

Did the floor judge fully evaluate the areas outlined in the manual? Yes _____ No _____

During the critique, did the floor judge provide, in a courteous and informative manner, the points that he or she thought were lacking in the team's performance, and did the floor judge offer suggestions or remedies for this? Yes _____ No _____

Lead Judge:

Was the lead judge available to answer any questions you may have had before the beginning of the competition? Yes _____ No _____

Did the lead judge resolve any conflicts with regard to the setup of the competition and the facilities? Yes _____ No _____

Did the tasting panel assist the floor judge with some of the duties? Yes _____ No _____

Was the critique attended by all the judges? Yes _____ No _____

Tasting Panel:

Were the individual critiques from each judge offered in a courteous and positive manner, and did the judges acknowledge the components of the meal that were good or outstanding? Yes _____ No _____

Did each judge explain why he or she thought that a particular error needed adjustment and what benefit could be achieved? Yes _____ No _____

Did each or any judge offer possible remedies or ideas on how to improve the dish and take it to the next level? Yes _____ No _____

Did any or all of the judges offer encouragement to the teams to keep trying to improve for future competitions? Yes _____ No _____

Comments:

Any other comments you may have that are critical or complimentary are welcomed.

Figure 10-4

Competitor/Coach Critique of Judges

The report shown in Figure 10-5 is to be filed by the chair of an ACF-approved culinary show and returned to the chair of the ACF's national Culinary Competition Committee within two weeks of the close of the show. In completing the report, the chair is expected to be thorough and specific, providing helpful comments on the performance of the host chapter, members of the judge's panel, and the national office as well.

The report shown in Figure 10-6 is to be filed by the head of the judges' panel of an ACF-approved culinary show and returned to the chair of the ACF's national Culinary Competition Committee within two weeks of the close of the show. Here, too, the head of the panel is asked to be thorough, specific, and helpful, providing comments on the performance of the host chapter, the show chair, and the national office.

COMPETITION SCORING

There are two areas of assessment in culinary competition scoring: the *score* and the *critique*.

The Score

When the judge's panel reviews a display, they award points in several categories, which are then averaged to yield a single score for the display. Based on a possible 40 points, displays are awarded gold, silver, or bronze medals. The ACF scoring point scale is:

Gold medal: 36–40 points

Silver medal: 32–35.99 points

Bronze medal 28–31.99 points

Unlike most competitions that typically have only one medal winner in each category, in ACF-sanctioned competitions, the competitors compete against a standard, not each other, so there may be multiple medal winners in each category. ACF medals are awarded to all competitors who score sufficient point levels in each medal category.

Competition categories are evaluated based on a number of criteria. By familiarizing yourself with this information, you'll come to understand what the judges look for and what is expected of you when you cook or display. Commonly, judges—myself included—begin by assuming the

ON THE MEDAL TRACK
A permanent record of every medal awarded is maintained at the ACF's national headquarters, located at 180 Center Place Way, St. Augustine, Florida, 32095.

General Information:

Show Chair: _____

Host Chapter: _____

Show Site/Name: _____

Show Dates: _____

Judges' Panel:
(Briefly describe the work of the members of the judge's panel. You may comment on their punctuality, thoroughness during the judging, and availability for critiques.)

Host Chapter:
(Briefly describe the host chapter's support in the production of the show. You may make recommendations/ suggestions for other chapters, particularly in areas where your chapter was successful.)

General Comments:
(Add any specific comments you have regarding this show not noted elsewhere. You may also draw on specifics about this show to illustrate a suggestion you may have for ACF-approved culinary shows in general.)

Signature: _____

Figure 10-5
Show Chair's Evaluation Report

General Information:

Lead Judge: _____

Host Chapter: _____

Show Site/Name: _____

Show Dates: _____

Show Administration:
Briefly describe the administration of the show—that is, how smoothly did it run? You may comment on the condition of the site and its suitability; how orderly was setup; were all the proper forms provided to the judges' panel; and were critiques held in an orderly fashion.

Protocol:
Briefly describe the host chapter's adherence to correct protocol. You may comment on hospitality services, including transportation, accommodations, and meals; attention to reimbursement of expenses; and assistance provided during the show.

General Comments:
Add any specific comments you have regarding this show not noted elsewhere. You may also draw on specifics about this show to illustrate a suggestion you may have for ACF-approved culinary shows in general.

Signature: _____

Figure 10-6
Lead Judge's Evaluation Report

best: that a competitor has adhered to the basics, employed proper slicing and cooking methods, and practiced proper sanitation procedures. They begin to deduct points only when these basics are not evident.

ASSESSMENT FOR CATEGORIES A, B, C, E, G

Displays in these categories are scored in several areas:

PRESENTATION AND GENERAL IMPRESSION: 10 POINTS

- Dishes should be appetizing and pleasing to the eye.
- Food should show flavor, to stimulate appetite.
- Glazing should show no beads or uneven aspic.
- Slices should be even, moderate.
- Portions should be correctly calculated and easily accessible.
- Plate or platter design should be modern, contemporary, and have customer service in mind.

COMPOSITION AND HARMONY OF INGREDIENTS: 10 POINTS

- Display must be nutritionally well balanced and in keeping with modern trends.
- Taste and colors should enhance each other, display practical craftsmanship, and be practical, digestible, and light.
- Seasonal ingredients should be used, and show flavor synergy.
- The theme should tie in with flavor profiles.
- Composition should take into account the enjoyment of the palate.
- Cooking methods should be apparent.

CORRECT PREPARATION AND CRAFTSMANSHIP: 15 POINTS

- Classical dish names should correspond to original recipes and methods of preparation.
- Preparations must display mastery of basic skills and application of proper cooking methods.
- Knife skills, cooking skills, and understanding of flavors should be demonstrated.

SERVING METHODS AND PORTIONS: 5 POINTS

- These should be simple and practical, enabling clean and careful serving, with no fuss.
- Overelaborate or impractical garnishing should not be in evidence.
- Garnishing should add value to the plate or display.
- Hot garnish should garnish hot food; cold garnish, cold food.
- Plate and platter arrangement should make for practical serving while maintaining a strong sense of elegance.

ASSESSMENT FOR CATEGORY D

Category D is for showpieces, hence competitors are expected to display more creativity than practicality, while conforming to certain standards. Showpieces must be made primarily of edible material; other materials should be reserved only for structural or support elements.

Showpieces are judged in four areas, each carrying a possible 10 points:

- Degree of difficulty
- Artistic achievement
- Work involved
- Originality

ASSESSMENT FOR CATEGORIES F AND G

The dynamics of judging category F, hot food competitions, are quite different from those used to judge other categories. In a cold food competition, the judging takes place in a display area, room, or hall, or is part of a trade show. A tabulator, the show chair, and several runners will be present. The competitors are absent, as are the public and the media until after the judging.

The assessment for category F is divided into two areas: kitchen/floor evaluation and service/tasting evaluation. These two areas are further divided into five more specific areas, which are scored individually. The total possible score (100 points) is divided by 2.5 to yield a medal score on a 40-point scale, as follows.

KITCHEN/FLOOR EVALUATION: 40 POSSIBLE POINTS
- Sanitation/food handling: 5 points
- Mise en place/organization: 5 points
- Culinary and cooking technique and proper execution: 20 points
- Proper utilization of ingredients: 5 points
- Timing/workflow: 5 points

SERVICE/TASTING EVALUATION: 60 POSSIBLE POINTS
- Serving methods and presentation: 5 points
- Portion size and nutritional balance: 5 points
- Menu and ingredient compatibility: 10 points
- Creativity and practicality: 5 points
- Flavor, taste, texture, and doneness: 35 points

ASSESSMENT FOR CATEGORIES K AND P/1, P/2:
HOT FOOD COOKING AND PATISSERIE TASTE-BASED JUDGING

The assessment for categories K and P/1 and P/2, hot food cooking and patisserie taste-based judging, is divided into three areas: organization, cooking skills and culinary techniques, and taste. Each of these areas is further divided into two or three specific areas, which are scored individually. There are 40 possible points.

ORGANIZATION: 10 POSSIBLE POINTS
- Sanitation/work habits: 5 points
- Utilization of ingredients and use of allotted time: 5 points

COOKING SKILLS AND CULINARY TECHNIQUES: 10 POSSIBLE POINTS
- Creativity, skills, craftsmanship: 5 points
- Serving, portion size: 5 points

TASTE: 20 POSSIBLE POINTS
- Flavor and texture: 10 points
- Ingredient compatibility, nutritional balance: 5 points
- Presentation: 5 points

ASSESSMENT FOR CATEGORY S:
SKILL-BASED JUDGING CRITIQUE AND SCORING

The assessment for category S is divided into three areas: organization, presentation, and workmanship. Each of these areas is further divided into two or three specific areas, which are scored individually. There are 40 possible points.

ORGANIZATION: 15 POSSIBLE POINTS
- Sanitation and product handling: 5 points
- Organization and mise en place: 5 points
- Workflow timing and follow-up: 5 points

PRESENTATION: 10 POSSIBLE POINTS
- Exactness, quality, quantity: 5 points
- Consistency, uniformity: 5 points

WORKMANSHIP: 15 POSSIBLE POINTS
- Knowledge of culinary skills and fundamentals: 5 points
- Proper use of ingredients and knife skills: 5 points
- Display of various techniques: 5 points

ASSESSMENT FOR CATEGORIES P/3–P/5:
PATISSERIE SKILL-BASED JUDGING CRITIQUE AND SCORING

The assessment for categories P/3–P/5 is divided into three areas: organization, presentation, and workmanship. Each of these areas is further divided into several specific areas, which are scored individually. Here, too, there are 40 possible points.

ORGANIZATION: **10** POSSIBLE POINTS
- Sanitation/work habits: 5 points
- Utilization of allotted time: 5 points

PRESENTATION: **10** POSSIBLE POINTS
- Overall impact of the display: 5 points
- Originality: 5 points

WORKMANSHIP: **20** POSSIBLE POINTS
- Use of various techniques: 5 points
- Uniformity: 5 points
- Exactness of skills displayed: 5 points
- Knowledge of skills displayed: 5 points

 ## CULINARY AWARDS

Culinary awards are made in the form of medals, diplomas, and certificates of participation:

Medals: Medals at the gold, silver, and bronze levels are available to ACF chapters sponsoring culinary competitions. These medals are applicable toward ACF certification. Scoring criteria are as follows: gold 36–40 points; silver 32–35.99 points; bronze 28–31.99 points. Following a competition, the sponsoring chapter forwards the judges' summary score sheets and payment for the medals to the national office. When this order is placed, the best effort is made to ship the awards the same day.

Culinary Diplomas: Culinary diplomas are issued with each medal and serve as verification for certification hours.

Certificates of Participation: These certificates are presented to competitors who do not qualify for a medal.

PROOF OF PARTICIPATION
Competitors must have a Certificate of Participation to receive points/hours toward ACF certification.

The Critique

I've spent a lot of time talking about how to score points and win medals, when in fact the most important "award" you can gain from a culinary competition is the education you receive. I want to stress this because, too often, I have seen competitors fail to take advantage of this aspect of competing. I recall judging a cook-off in which a first-, second-, or third-place winner would be named, including cash prizes, along with any ACF medals earned. Unfortunately, there were no outstanding food entries at this cook-off, yet due to the sponsorship and contest, the cash awards had to be given. We ended up awarding a bronze medal (barely) for first and two diplomas for second and third. Not one of the contestants stayed around after the judging; they only came to the awards presentations, collected their checks, and left. Not to stay and take the time to speak with the judges and ask what went wrong, and what they could do to improve their work, showed a lack of commitment to the craft; and they threw away an opportunity to raise their personal culinary standard. If you take no interest in the education process, you will never become a true culinary craftsman.

As I mentioned at the beginning of this chapter, another benefit to entering ACF-sponsored competitions is that the judges are required to be available for the feedback sessions; it is mandatory on the part of the show host to ensure this happens. Many other competitions do not enforce this. ACF judges are also trained to give feedback that is constructive and based on solid cooking principles (not opinions). The goal is to make competitors feel good about their efforts, yet learn exactly what they need to do to improve the next time. There is simply no substitute for a professional, constructive critique or feedback, when it is delivered with the respect afforded to a professional colleague.

Critique sessions are normally held immediately following the judging session and before the opening of the show for public viewing. This not only makes it possible for the judge and the competitor to discuss his or her display privately, but by having the critique as soon as possible after viewing by the judges' panel, the display is still fresh in judges' minds, resulting in critiques that are accurate, and hence more meaningful and helpful to the competitor.

WHEN STUDENTS COMPETE

When a competitor is a student, his or her instructor should be present during the critique. That said, the instructor should support the judge's feedback, to avoid dissention. Obviously, if a student does not perform or display well, it generally is a reflection on the coaching and teaching process, so in a very real sense, the coach as well as the student is receiving the feedback, and both can and should learn from it. I remember once giving feedback to a young team of culinarians who really needed to make some fundamental improvements on the buffet. After spending much time with the team to ensure that every effort was made to assist them, the instructor pulled them aside and told them not to worry, that the judges did not know what they were talking about. This was an injustice to the students, and only served to confuse them and, worse, misguide them.

The best critiques are to the point, noting both strong and weak points, with specifics about each. In addition, the critiquing judge should offer guidance as to which skills and techniques could or should be developed further.

To get the most from your critique, I recommend the following:

- Take very good notes, especially in regard to the items cited as needing improvement. Consider bringing a small tape recorder for this purpose.
- Focus on the feedback that gives you quantifiable, tangible instruction for improving your display, the flavor of your food, and/or the way you work.
- Do not be afraid to ask questions. If there is a technique you would like to know about, ask.
- Do not argue about classical techniques or try to introduce your "version." If you say you are cooking Sole Veronique, there is no "my version"; there is only the classical preparation, period.
- Take pictures of your entries and keep a file from show to show so you can measure your own improvement.
- Do not compare yourself to another competitor. Perhaps that person was awarded a gold and you the silver, but there is also the chance that your silver was only a half-point from the gold. At the end of the day, it does not matter, as you are judged against the criteria: that is the beauty of an ACF competition. In ACF competitions, you are measured against yourself, nobody else.

 ## CONCLUSION

I hope this chapter has given you valuable insight to the judging and scoring processes as established by the American Culinary Federation. By understanding all participants in the culinary competition arena, you can and will become a "seasoned competitor." In the next chapter, you will learn about one more important "player": the competition host.

CHAPTER

11

Hosting an ACF Competition

As you might imagine, hosting any competition is a big commitment, organizing and hosting an ACF competition is even more so. ACF takes pride in its shows and try's to ensure that each show is organized, follows correct protocol and is of a high standard. Therefore, it is imperative that the host chapter or group understand in advance their commitment, which is to provide competitors and judges alike with an environment that is responsive to the needs and goals of a culinary competition. As a competitor, it is important as well to understand what it takes to launch a show of this type, as this will increase your appreciation of the experience. This book is for ACF members who compete, want to compete and who may host a show.

Beyond the obvious—making sure the competition venue is safe, secure, and first-class—when it comes to hosting, attending to details is top priority for, inevitably, it is the little things that make for a big-picture success.

For cold competitions:

■ Is the air conditioning adequate to keep the room at 50 degrees Fahrenheit, so the displays stay fresh?

■ Are the tables lined with quality linens? Is there a sign-in area for the competitors to receive their cards and to assist them with any concerns?

■ Is the lighting proper so the displays pop out? Is the area roped off to keep the public from touching or getting to close until after all the judging is complete?

■ For hot food contest have you followed the guidelines completely? Have you made sure that the work stations are first class and provide the competitor a great kitchen and venue in cooking environment?

■ Will the public and the press look at the kitchen and say, "Wow!—nice setup"? Have you made arrangements to sell tickets or invite VIP guests to dine and taste the food if it is a basket or multicourse meal?

■ Have you ensured the sponsorship is one of integrity and a win-win for

TABLE 11-1   Minimum Requirements for a Hot Food Competition

Kitchen Station Requirements	Judges' Table Requirements
Small oven, Farberware or Baker's Pride, convection or conventional	Silverware, napkins, water, glasses
Cook top, minimum two burners: induction, electric, or gas	Large clock in competition area for accurate time-keeping
Worktable	Competitor staging area for ingredient check-in by the judges
Marble slab*	Copies of recipes, a full set from each competitor, for each judge
Kitchen-Aid-type mixer*	Complete starting time schedules
Cutting boards	All taste- and skill-based score sheets and tally sheets, complete with competitor information
Access to refrigeration (can be shared)	Scorekeepers to assist judges
Power supply, four outlets per station	Clipboards, pads, pencils, pens, calculators, and staplers
Cubed ice, ice supply	
Generic white china plates, various shapes and sizes (if available)	
Garbage receptacles; brooms, mops, and buckets; bleach	
Hot and cold water sanitation station in immediate vicinity	
Paper towels, plastic wrap, foil	
Measuring scale, measuring in ounces and pounds.	

*Applies to pastry kitchens only.

144

all parties concerned: the organizers, the sponsor, and most of all the competitors?

- Have the best judges for the competition been secured?
- Have travel and hotel accommodations for judges been arranged?

In general, more is required to host a hot food competition than a cold. Table 11-1 lists the minimum requirements needed to host a contemporary hot food competition.

PROPER CARE OF JUDGES

ACF judges give of their time and energy; they take time off from their jobs and away from their families to officiate at culinary competitions. They do this to "give back" to professional colleagues. Therefore, a show host should do everything possible (but within reason) to make their attendance as trouble-free and comfortable as possible, from making all travel arrangements (including pickup at airports or train stations) to booking pleasant and convenient accommodations and allowing for reasonable expenses (such as room service if no dinner was arranged, or even a movie after a long day to say thank you). Similarly, it's important to consider scheduling: Don't overwhelm the judges with events, so that they don't have time to rest and check in on their work and families.

This all may seem obvious, but ACF judges give of their time, take off from their jobs to judge a contest and some times spend one to three days away from work and family. I have seen small chapters take care of a judge with VIP treatment and larger ones not even have the hotel accommodations ready when a judge arrives. There was one contest where the judges were placed at a Motel 6 while the chapter and their members where at the Hilton the host hotel for the show. I have seen large money prizes given and a show make a nice pay day for the chapter or restaurant association or exhibit company who runs the show while the top judges do not receive a dime for their efforts and days away from work.

Many judges do not have their own business and take personal days off just to judge and give back. It is also important that judges do not take advantage of the show, misuse any privileges, overcharge expenses on the room, constantly spend time during the competition on their cell phone, and leave before feedback and critique sessions.

This needs to be reported to the lead judge, the ACF national office, and a complete feedback form needs to be filled out and sent in to the office and competition committee chair. Yes it is much work and effort and organizing to host an ACF competition, but the awards of giving back and allowing a venue for chefs, cooks, and culinarians to display their talents, educate and learn from all involved is as they say priceless!

The following pages will indeed give you all the information needed to host and organize a first-class show.

BEHIND THE SCENES OF AN ACF CULINARY COMPETITION

The American Culinary Federation approves approximately 80 culinary competitions each year, ranging from small contests with fewer than a dozen competitors to national shows where displays number in the hundreds. All of these shows are sponsored by local ACF chapters.

For the ACF to sanction a culinary competition, the nature of the competition must be assessed to ensure compliance with organizational standards. In addition, the application to host (see Figure 11-1) is scrutinized by the chair of the Culinary Competition Committee (CCC) to verify the proper assignment of judges to monitor the competition.

For a culinary competition to be sanctioned by the ACF, three basic criteria must be met:

- The competition must be sponsored and administered by a local ACF chapter in good standing.
- The competition must adhere to the guidelines described in this chapter, including category requirements, award system, and judging criteria.
- The judge's panel must include a minimum of three ACF-approved culinary judges, one of whom must have international show experience, and one pastry chef, if necessary.

TIP

Current listings of ACF-approved culinary judges are available for download from the ACF Web site or from the ACF's Events Management Department. The Events Management Department will work closely with the show chair to ensure the competition is a success from the planning stages through the awarding of medals.

Application Procedure

The application process for an ACF-sanctioned competition begins at least six months before the competition, when an application is filed for approval with the ACF national office (see Figure 11-1). Failure to begin the process at least six months before the competition date may result in a competition not receiving approval.

There are two reasons necessitating the lengthy lead time:

- To allow adequate processing time of the application by the show chair, national office, and the chair of the CCC.
- To meet advance publishing deadlines so that the show may be advertised in *The National Culinary Review/Center of the Plate*

Application to Host an ACF Show

Host Chapter: _____

Show Dates: _____ to _____

Application Procedures
For a culinary show to receive ACF approval:
• It must be sponsored and administered by a local ACF chapter in good standing;
• It must adhere to the latest edition of the *Culinary Competition Manual.*
• The judge's panel must have a minimum of three ACF-approved culinary judges, one of whom must have international show experience, and one of whom is a pastry chef. Additional judges may be required for larger hot food competitions. The lead judge in ice carving competitions must be an ACF-approved ice judge. (Additional use of one apprentice judge is strongly recommended.)

Administrative Requirements
Four months (minimum) before show, the chapter show chair must submit a completed application packet, to include:
• A completed application form
• Copies of letters from each invited judge verifying his or her commitment to judge
• Letter explaining judge's protocol
• A $200 application fee

Send completed applications to:
  Events Management Department, American Culinary Federation
  180 Center Place Way
  St. Augustine, FL 32095

FOR OFFICE USE ONLY
DATE RECEIVED:
NOTES:

_____
_____
_____
_____

Application Information
The mailing address below will be used for all competition-related correspondence and the shipping of awards. Only those phone numbers indicated will be made available to the public (*The National Culinary Review,* ACF Web site, press releases, etc.).

Show Chair Name: _____

Mailing Address: _____

City: _____

State: _____ Zip: _____

Home Phone: _____

Business Phone: _____

Fax: _____

(continues)

Figure 11-1
Host Application

E-mail: _____

Indicate which numbers can be released: [ ] Home [ ] Business [ ] Fax [ ] E-mail

Secondary Contact Name: _____

Phone: _____ (Phone number will not be released)

Show Information

Show Site: _____

Mailing Address: _____

City: _____ State: _____ Zip: _____

Contact Name: _____

Business Phone: _____

Fax: _____

E-mail: _____

Setup Date: _____ Time: _____

Breakdown Date: _____ Time: _____

Categories

Cold Food:
- [ ] A— Cookery
- [ ] B—Cookery
- [ ] C—Pastry/Confections
- [ ] D—Culinary Art (Showpieces)
- [ ] E—Team Buffet

Hot Food:
- [ ] F/1—Mystery Basket, Professional
- [ ] F/2—Mystery Basket, Student
- [ ] F/3—Regional Taste/Customized
- [ ] F/4—Nutritional Hot Food
- [ ] F/5—Pastry Mystery Basket

Edible Cold Food:
- [ ] G—Edible Cold Food

Student Team National Championship:
- [ ] Local/State Competition
- [ ] Regional Competition

Practical & Contemporary Hot Food:
- [ ] K/1—Game Hen, Chicken, or Duck
- [ ] K/2—Bone-in Pork Loin
- [ ] K/3—Bone-in Veal Loin or Rack
- [ ] K/4—Bone-in Lamb Loin or Rack
- [ ] K/5—Game Birds
- [ ] K/6—Bone-in Game
- [ ] K/7—Whole Rabbit
- [ ] K/8—Live Lobster
- [ ] K/9—Fish

Practical & Contemporary—Skill-Based:
- [ ] S/1—Vegetables

Figure 11-1
Host Application *(continued)*

Practical & Contemporary Patisserie:
[ ] P/1—Hot/Warm Dessert
[ ] P/2—Composed Cold Dessert
[ ] P/3—Cake Decoration
[ ] P/4—Marzipan Modeling
[ ] P/5—Decorative Centerpiece
Ice Carving:
[ ] H/1—Single block, Individual freestyle, three hours
[ ] H/2—Two-person team, three blocks, three hours
[ ] H/3—Three-person team, five blocks, three hours
[ ] H/4—Two- or three-person team, 15-20 blocks, 48 hours

In the space below, describe any non-ACF categories that may be included in the competition. Also use this space for further explanation of the categories noted.

_____
_____
_____
_____
_____
_____

ACF-Approved Judges (Minimum of Three)

_____
_____
_____
_____
_____
_____

Verification:
To the best of my knowledge, all information in this application is true and accurate. Our chapter agrees to meet all financial obligations related to this competition and distribute awards in a timely manner.

Signature of show chair
_____   Date: _____
Signature of host chapter president
_____   Date: _____

FOR OFFICE USE ONLY

Approval
_____
National Culinary Competition Committee Chair
_____   Date: _____
Notes/comments:
_____
Lead judge
_____

and so that competition information can be included on the ACF Web site (www.acfchefs.org) as soon as possible.

Culinary Competition Timeline

MEDAL INFORMATION
Chapters wishing to order medals in advance must submit a request, in writing, stating the type and quantity of medals required. This request must be accompanied by a deposit of 50 percent of the total cost of medals being shipped. The following awards and certificates are available: professional medals with diplomas, ice-carving, and junior medals. (Current pricing information is available by calling the ACF National Office, (904)824-4468).

For any show to run smoothly, it is necessary to follow a precompetition "task timeline," as follows:

- **Five Months Before:** Chapter show chair fills out a culinary competition application and obtains the required chapter officer signatures.
- **Four Months Before:** The show chair submits the following to the Events Management Department:
  - ☐ Completed application form
  - ☐ Letters of commitment from three ACF-approved culinary judges agreeing to judge the competition
  - ☐ Letter stating the protocol for handling judges, to include who is charged with making their travel arrangements and other accommodations, and stating any payments or stipends.
  - ☐ A $200 application fee
- **Three Months Before:** Applications are reviewed and forwarded to the chair of the Culinary Competition Committee for approval and the designation of a lead judge. Competition information is posted on the ACF Web site and forwarded to *The National Culinary Review/Center of the Plate* for publication.
- **Two Months Before:** Approval status is forwarded by letter from the ACF National Office to chapter show chair.

It's also important to establish a detailed schedule for the duration of the competition. Here's a sample:

	START TIME	PLATE/JUDGING	CLEANUP/OUT BY
Competition #1:	8:00 a.m.	9:00-9:05	9:25
Competition #2:	8:10 a.m.	9:10-9:15	9:35
Competition #3:	8:20 a.m.	9:20-9:25	9:45
Competition #4:	8:30 a.m.	9:30-9:35	9:55
Competition #5:	8:40 a.m.	9:40-9:45	10:05

Expand as needed, for number of customers

Following the competition, too, task timing is important. The week after the competition, the show chair should submit to the Events Management Department the following:

- Original copies of the signed judges' Summary Score Sheets. When listing team events, a list of all team members should be submitted.
- Payment for medals. (Best effort is made to ship awards within three working days of receipt of the order.)
- Thank-you letters to judges and volunteers.

One month after the competition, the show chair distributes awards to competitors, if they were not presented at the time of the competition.

Competition Organizational Structure

Every culinary event requires a staff organizational structure. Though many chapters rely on the show chairperson to organize and conduct the entire competition, this is really feasible only for small shows. It is not recommended for moderate to large-scale competitions, where a division of labor is necessary and teamwork is the key to success.

Because every culinary competition is different, there is no "standard" organizational structure that can be implemented. What works for one chapter may not work for others. Everything, from personalities, talent, and experience must be factored in, to ensure a smooth-running system. That said, some general guidelines can be drawn, and these are shown in Table 11-2.

In addition, most show hosts will include a marketing/publicity person and an awards/scoring assistant to the structural mix, to handle the following responsibilities:

MARKETING/PUBLICITY
- Reports to show chair
- Distributes details of competition to target media
- Prepares and distributes pre- and postcompetition press releases

AWARDS/SCORING ASSISTANT
- Reports to show chair
- Coordinates applications/registration for show participation
- Supports judges during competition
- Assigns scorekeeping assistants, starters, timekeepers
- Provides score sheets
- Tabulates and verifies scoring
- Tracks awards and ensures recipients receive them in a timely manner

TABLE 11-2   Typical Competition Division of Labor

Chapter President	Show Chair	Kitchen Manager	Protocol Manager
Overall responsibility for conduct of the competition and actions of the chapter.	Reports to chapter president.	Reports to show chair.	Reports to show chair.
Signs application and authorizes chapter sponsorship.	Serves as main point of contact internally and externally.	Secures and arranges delivery of all required kitchen equipment and food products for the competition.	Secures the best judges for the show; also arranges their transportation and accommodations and then follows through so that the VIPs/judges are supported and cared for in a proper manner which includes all transportation and pick-ups, lodging of quality and meals, coffee, danish, water and soft drinks waiting at show, lab coats with logo or ask the judges to bring their own.
Determines format and extent of competition and chapter capability to support it.	Responsible for assisting the chapter president in overall coordination and management of all details of the competition.	Serves as main kitchen area safety supervisor. Arranges fire watches and other facility safety requirements.	Arranges for per diem support for large shows, money shows, and NRA or other large company-sponsored shows (a diem of $150 to $250 a day is suggested).
Appoints/directs the show chair.	Appoints/directs assistants, as necessary.	Monitors and refreshes judges' tasting equipment and refreshments.	Takes care of thank-you notes, postshow. (Commercial sponsors of competition should be recognized.)
Ensures postcompetition follow-up.			
Handles award payments/presentations.			
Validates travel/per diem payments.			
Facilitates payment of invoices/bills.			

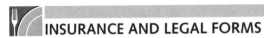

INSURANCE AND LEGAL FORMS

Insurance and legal forms to use are shown in Figures 11–2 and 11–3.

Wavier of liability /and agreement of indemnity between Competitor: _____ and
Chapter/sponsor: _____. The
undersigned acknowledges that he/she has requested and made formal application for participation in
the_____ sponsored by _____. I understand
that participation in said competition will involve the use of chain saws and other articles of equipment necessary to
shape and sculpt blocks of ice weighing in excess of 400 pounds. In consideration for and as a condition of being
permitted to participate for any purpose in this event, each of the undersigned, for himself or herself and personal
representatives, assign, heirs, and next of kin, agrees that he or she has or will have before his or her participation in
the event sponsored by _____ .
_____ acknowledge that he/she can fully participate in all areas the competi-
tion will encompass without restriction, that he/she is fully aware of the responsibilities his or her participation will
require and the dangers wherein thereto, and does further warrant that his/her participation constitutes an acknowl-
edgment that he or she has inspected the location where the competition is to be held and the equipment to be used
and that both are safe and reasonably suited for their intended purposes. In addition, the _____
_____ (all sponsors) will not be responsible for theft or damage to any personal property,
tools, or equipment before, during, or after the event. Therefore, the undersigned hereby voluntarily releases, waives,
discharges, and covenants not to sue the _____ (all sponsors),
its officers, directors, employees, or agents all for purposes herein referred to as Releases, from all liability to the
undersigned, his or her personal representative, assigns, heirs, and next of kin for all loss or damage and any claim or
demands therefore, on account of injury to the person or property or resulting in death of the undersigned, whether
caused by the negligence of the Releasee or otherwise, from participation in the event referred to above.

Signatures:

_____ (Contestant's Name)

_____ (ACF Chapter/Sponsor's Name)

Date _____

Figure 11-2
Hold Harmless Agreement

Please print or write clearly.

Date of Request: _____

Person completing this form: _____

Name of insured: _____

Chapter Name/Number, if applicable: _____

Address: _____

Phone No.: (_____)_____ Fax. No. (___)_____

Describe Event: _____

Date(s): _____

Location Address: _____

Entity requesting proof of your coverage (NOT YOU—you are the Named Insured)

Name of Certificate Holder: _____

Attention: _____

Address: _____

Phone No. (_____)_____

Fax. No. (_____)_____

Does the Certificate Holder require special coverage, such as Additional Insured? Yes ___ No _____
Additional Insured: You should avoid adding another party as Additional Insured when possible.
We can verify that you have insurance coverage without adding another party as an Additional Insured.
_____ Yes _____ No If you entered into any written agreement, contract, or permit, a copy of the document(s) or contract must be provided to us with this certificate request. If it is not provided, the certificate CANNOT be issued.
Mail the original certificate directly to the Certificate Holder? Yes ___ No ____
Fax the certificate to the Certificate Holder? Yes _____ No ____
A copy will be faxed to you unless otherwise requested. Yes _____ No ____

PLEASE ALLOW AT LEAST 48 HOURS TO PROCESS THIS REQUEST.
PLEASE COMPLETE AND RETURN TO:
    Aon Association Services
    A Division of Affinity Insurance Services, Inc.
    1120 20th Street, NW, 6th floor
    Washington, DC 20036-3406
    Toll-Free: 800-453-5191 ext. 349 or 202-862-5349; Fax: 202-223-4080

Figure 11-3
Certificate of Insurance Request Form

CONCLUSION

Yes, it takes a lot of work to host an ACF competition, but the rewards—in the form of giving back and providing a venue for chefs, cooks, and culinarians to display their talents and learn from all involved—as they say, are priceless!

Building a Pastry Display

A pastry display of any kind, shape, or size should show multiple levels of your thought process and skills. To address this competition category, I asked my colleague Chef Thomas Vaccaro, who led the ACF Culinary Team USA at the IKA in Germany in 2004 and was team pastry chef at ScotHot in 2001, for his insights.

As you know by now, not all competitions are created equal, so the first piece of advice Chef Vaccaro offers is to always read the rules first, carefully. If some of the guidelines are not clear to you, get answers before you proceed. Contact the competition chair for help, if necessary. When you are ready to start the thought process of your display, "hit the books." Use all resources available to you for research and inspiration: the Internet, libraries, bookstores, and museums; and don't forget to ask other professional chefs for their opinions of your ideas.

Your display should eventually become a part of your everyday life. This may sound extreme, but because your display will represent your work as a professional chef, you must give it all you've got. When you are ready to start putting your ideas on paper, collect your reference materials. They should be readily available so that you can check quickly and easily that your display is accurate in design and theme.

First drawings from an aesthetic point of view—by which he means your display should be a clear representation of the theme. Attempt to maintain proportions of size, shape, color, and texture; and aim to evoke a warm, inviting feel from the display. When a judge looks at your display for the first time, he or she should be able to discern the theme immediately. Then the judge should be able to interpret the impact of your choice of media—textures, colors, shapes, and proportions. At all times, the judge should be able to clearly interpret your intent.

Chef Vaccaro recommends that the display should have a good "dose" of reality—unless, of course, your intent is a totally abstract design. Remember, aesthetics are the first value given to your display.

When you are ready to start designing your flavors, use those that have worked for you in the past. That means use flavor combinations that you have tasted and you know work well together. For his flavor profiles, Chef Vaccaro usually prefers strong flavors, such as caramel, raspberry, citrus, chocolate, and nuts. He does incorporate exotic flavors, but in small portions.

Variety is important, too. Use as many techniques and skills as you can. Do not repeat flavors, shapes, sauces, garnishes, and certain baking preparations. (Size is the one exception: Try to keep your portion size consistent throughout the display.) One of the most common mistakes contestants make is to repeat flavors, techniques, or garnishes, or to overutilize a particular ingredient (e.g., fruit, nuts, spices, chocolate, coffee, dairy products, reductions, vanilla, sugars, and herbs). Diversify techniques, as well, such as cold process mousses, baked items, poached, caramelized, glazed, jams, fried, sabbayons, frozen, semifrozen, sautéed, and grilled. Garnishes should also show many different flavors and skills (e.g., candied fruits, tuile, croquant, sugar, chocolates, meringues, fondants, butter cream, whipped cream, crème fraiche, dried fruits, fried garnishes, etc.) In short, use all available resources for flavor combinations and appeal. (Vaccaro recommends many of the published dessert books available today.)

When you have completed your program on paper, you can begin the process of refining your thoughts by practicing. Chef Vaccaro likes to practice at least six times before presenting his displays. And whatever the size of your program, your first practice should be the entire program. The display should represent what you have collected in your notes. When practicing, document all recipes, sizes, equipment needs, and temperatures as you work. If you do not have the time to produce your centerpiece, use a close representation of it so that you can achieve perspective on height and shape for your overall program. Vaccaro suggests using foamboard or cardboard and a hot glue gun to assemble your piece.

When you have completed your first practice session, take pictures and process them as soon as possible (digital cameras are great for this purpose). Write any additional notes and attach them to your collected data. At this stage, your program may not be what you drew on paper, but stay the course and keep refining.

For the next practice session, invite an accomplished chef-competitor who has participated in the same or a similar competition to the one you are entering. Have the guest chef judge your work as if it were competition day. Remember, the tougher the critique, the better you will become. When you are reviewing the critique of the guest chef, read it carefully and follow the advice given. That said, don't be afraid to trust your own feelings about your work.

The final presentation of your practiced display should follow a timeline leading up to displaying your presentation. (If, however, you are entering a timed competition, you should be practicing timelines from the first practice.)

When delivering sugar pieces, keep in mind the following:

- Adjust the temperature in your shop. Extreme temperature changes will crack your piece.
- Don't overhandle chocolate pieces.
- Keep the piece clean of fingerprints, smudges, and scrapes.
- Build Styrofoam boxes to hold fragile pieces. This will insulate and act as a shock absorber.
- Bring backups of garnishes, sauces, and very fragile pieces to the show.
- Take a test ride to the show venue, and find the best route to take.
- Pack a box of equipment, to include knives, spatulas, torch, towels, water, backup sugar and chocolate, and so on.

If you follow these guidelines, on the day of the show you should be ready, and confident that your display will meet the requirements of the competition. Practice, determination, discipline, and desire to win will help to make your display a success.

Rules and Guidelines for ACF Competitions

A s one of the largest organizers of culinary competitions, there are many benefits to participating in an American Culinary Federation–approved show. Primary among those benefits is that the ACF offers a wide variety of shows to select from, covering every aspect of culinary skills from pastry, garde, hot food, and more. And thanks to its point system, when participants compete in an ACF show, they compete primarily against themselves. If, for example, there are six chefs competing, it is possible for all six chefs to receive a gold medal, should their work score as such. The ACF also guarantees that its rules and guidelines are consistent throughout the country and are based on understandable and universal criteria. Moreover, along with gaining valuable experience and education, which are the greatest rewards of competing, participants are awarded points for certification or recertification.

ACF judges are given clear guidelines to follow when evaluating each of the competition categories (defined below). ACF's approved judges list is reviewed and updated yearly; and to maintain its high-level judging list, the ACF provides mandatory training for all potential judges.

ACF WORLDWIDE SCOPE

The ACF is a member of the World Association of Cooks Society (WACS), which sets the standards for worldwide competitions. ACF counts among its members American chefs who have been approved both as ACF and international judges. And as the main sponsor for Culinary Team USA, which competes in the worldwide arena, the ACF hosts the tryouts.

Finally, the ACF offers comprehensive information to anyone interested in competing or hosting a show in its manual (regularly updated to include new standards of cuisine and industry changes). And announcements of upcoming culinary shows are listed in the *National Culinary Review* and on the ACF Web site, www.acfchefs.org.

The purpose of this chapter is to detail the current guidelines, standards, and rules for the ACF competition categories.

TRADITIONAL COMPETITION CATEGORIES

There are 10 traditional competition categories, identified by the letters A-H, K, and P, with certain of these categories containing subdivisions, which are further identified by a number (e.g, A-1, B-3, F/1, P/5).

Category A: Cooking, Professional and Student

In this category, show platters need to be a minimum of eight portions on the platter and one portion on a display plate. The competitor must demonstrate at least two protein items, two garnishes, one salad, and the appropriate sauce, as follows:

[Select One—All items must be properly glazed]

- A-1 Cold platter of meat, beef, veal, lamb, or pork
- A-2 Cold platter of fish and/or shellfish
- A-3 Cold platter of poultry
- A-4 Cold platter of game
- A-5 One cold hors d'oeuvres selection, with a minimum of eight varieties, served with appropriate sauces and garnishes

Category B: Cooking, Professional and Student (Hot Food Presented Cold)

This is a gastronomique menu, implying a special occasion, holiday, or a special dinner; or referring to a contemporary style of fine dining tasting menu. The theme should be carried throughout all dishes.

[Select one—All items must be properly glazed]

- B-1 Six different cold appetizer plates
- B-2 Six different hot appetizer plates, presented cold

- B-3 One five-course tasting menu gastronomique for one person, prepared hot and presented cold, comprising two appetizers, one consommé, one salad, and one entree all within proper tasting portions and contemporary presentations
- B-4 One restaurant platter for four persons prepared hot but displayed cold, and one vegetarian platter for two prepared hot but displayed cold

Category C: Patisserie/Confectionery, Professional and Student

To complete this category, all requirements must be displayed and all exhibited pieces must be made of edible materials.
[Select one]

- C-1 Decorated celebration cake—sugar paste, rolled fondant, or royal icing; any shape with a maximum display area of 15 by 15 inches; no dummy cakes are permitted
- C-2 One buffet platter of fancy cookies, chocolates, or petits fours (platter must be made up of eight varieties, eight portions each) with one plate for tasting
- C-3 Six different individual hot or cold desserts (must be prepared as an individual plated serving), and all shown cold
- C-4 Wedding cake: at least three tiers with a maximum display area of 36 by 36 inches; no dummy cakes are permitted
- C-5 Novelty cake: imaginative creation in shape and design; cake and decorations must be edible

Category D: Showpieces

The exhibits in this category should demonstrate the difference between cookery and culinary art. The use of commercial molds is not permitted.
[Select one]

- D-1 Tallow or carving: a maximum display area of 30 by 30 inches; no external supports are allowed
- D-2 Saltillage: a maximum display area of 30 by 30 inches; no external supports are allowed
- D-3 Pastillage: maximum display area of 30 by 30 inches; no external supports are allowed
- D-4 Chocolate: maximum display area of 30 by 30 inches; no external supports are allowed

- D-5 Marzipan: maximum display area of 24 by 24 inches; no supports are allowed
- D-6 Cooked sugar: maximum display area of 30 by 30 inches; no supports are allowed

Category E: Team Buffet

This category requires a team of four chefs. Maximum display area is 12 by 10 feet, and the buffet must include:

- Six different appetizers, one portion each
- A plated seven-course meal for one person
- A show platter of meat, poultry, or game
- A show platter of fish or seafood
- Six different plated desserts
- One buffet platter of fancy cookies, chocolates, or petits fours (platter must be made up of eight varieties, eight portions each); one plate for tasting

Category F: Hot Food Competition

Hot food competitions are events at which competitors cook and present food to be judged on taste as well as execution of skills and presentation. These competitions require more organization, work, and commitment than cold food competitions, in that kitchen space is required; raw products must be provided and monitored; and student helpers, proctors, and servers must be provided.

Hot food competitions that make use of the Mystery Basket (see Chapter 9) are the best for displaying the skills required of chefs and cooks. Signature dish competitions are often used in larger events as a preliminary event to narrow the field. Other competitions combine aspects of both, requiring a signature event for the entrée and a Mystery Basket for the appetizer, soup, salad, and dessert. It is also possible to have a signature appetizer, followed by a Mystery Basket for the salad, main plate, and dessert. As noted in Chapter 9, ingredients for the Mystery Basket will vary in each competition, but they must always be the same for each competitor and must never be revealed in advance. The basket must be designed by the lead judge for the competition. For an individual competition, food will be needed for 4 courses and 10 portions. The community kitchen at these events is stocked, minimally, with the products listed in Table 13-1.

TABLE 13-1   Minimum Community Storeroom Products

Produce	Groceries	Spices and Seasonings	Fresh Herbs
Carrots	Dijon-style mustard	Selection	Minimum five
Celery	Gelatin (powder and sheet)	**Flour**	**Stocks**
Garlic	Three essential oils	All-purpose flour/ bread flour	Chicken
Baking potatoes	Sugar	Cornmeal flour	Fish
Onions (Spanish and Bermuda)	Soy sauce	Whole wheat flour	Brown veal
Root vegetables	Tabasco style sauce	**Dairy**	**Pastry Items**
Shallots	Teriyaki sauce	Butter	Brown sugar
Lettuce, two varieties	Tomato paste or puree	Cream	Powdered sugar
Tomatoes	Worcestershire	Cream cheese	Vanilla beans
Fruits	Vinegar	Milk	Cocoa powder
Minimum: three seasonal	Wines, red and white	Sour cream	Almonds
Lemons	Brandy	Yogurt	Corn syrup
Limes	**Rice**	Eggs	High-gluten flour
Oranges	Short and long grain	Margarine	Milk chocolate
Staples	White		Dark chocolate
Cornstarch			Shortening
Barley			
Bread crumbs			
Cornmeal			
Bread			

CATEGORY F/1: HOT FOOD, PROFESSIONAL

In this category, each competitor will have four hours to prepare 10 servings of a three- or four-course menu. Of the 10 portions to be prepared:

- Three are for judge tasting.
- One is for photos, critiques and the press.
- Six are for individual plated service and/or platter service.

CATEGORY F/2: HOT FOOD, STUDENT

The same rules and procedures apply to students and apprentices as to their professional counterparts in hot food competition, with the exception that each student competitor prepares a three-course meal of 10 portions each, including a starter, main course, and dessert. The meal plan should demonstrate, first and foremost, basic culinary preparation skills, as well as regional and national cooking techniques.

CATEGORY F/3: REGIONAL TASTES/CUSTOMIZED COMPETITION

Many competitions in the F/3 category are sponsored and are a great way to gain experience and win prizes. Local ACF chapters and other organizations wishing to sponsor hot food competitions that are sponsor-driven or do not follow the prescribed Mystery Basket, contemporary format, or cold food competitions may apply for ACF approval. The standard application must be supplemented with a detailed description of the competition and be submitted a full six months before the competition. It must have the approval of the Culinary Competition Committee chair. Specialty competitions can also be organized (e.g., wild mushrooms, asparagus, seasonal artichoke, squash, specialty produce), provided their purpose is to demonstrate specific skills.

CATEGORY F/4: NUTRITIONAL HOT FOOD CHALLENGE

This unique competition format is ideal for strengthening the established alliance with a registered dietitian. This category requires the development of a four-course meal plan (i.e., appetizers, soup or salad, entree, and dessert) for a total of 10 portions. Competitors have four hours cooking time.

The following preliminaries are to be completed before the competition:

- Completed entry documents
- Typed recipes for the four-course meal plan
- A color photograph of each dish in the meal
- Nutritional analysis for each course, and the meal plan approved by a registered dietitian

Criteria for the selection of cook-off finalists will be based on submitted recipes. A selection committee, designated by the show chair in charge of organizing the competition, will use the following standardized format for the evaluation and selection of eligible competitors. In addition, the selection committee must be composed of equal numbers of professional chefs and registered dietitians. Each criterion will be assigned a point value of 20 points. Criteria for the selection of finalists are:

- Incorporation of the principles of moderation and balance as identified in *The 1990 Dietary Guidelines for America*, published by the U. S. Department of Agriculture and U.S. Department of Health and Human Services. The overall meal plan should contain a maximum of 1,000 calories with: 50 percent of calories from carbohydrates; 30 percent or less of calories from fat; 20 percent of calories from protein. The overall meal plan should contain no more than: 150 mg. cholesterol and 1,500 mg. sodium.
- Evaluation of the total meal plan as a part of a healthful diet on the basis of nutritional adequacy, performed by a registered dietitian.
- Use of a variety of ingredients and culinary preparation techniques to yield optimal nutrition.
- Assessment of culinary creativity and composition to enhance appearance.

THE RIGHT STUFF

The nutritional analysis must be confirmed and completed by the registered dietitian and presented in the form of a letter stating that the meal plan was evaluated for overall nutritional adequacy and meets the nutritional guidelines required for the competition. The letter must also specify which software program was used for the analysis.

CATEGORY F/5: PASTRY MYSTERY BASKET

Each competitor will have three hours to prepare 10 servings of three plated desserts. Of the 10 portions to be prepared:

- Three are for judge tasting.
- One is for photos, critiques, and the press.
- Six are for individual plated service and/or platter service.

Similar to the communal kitchen in the hot food Mystery Basket, a communal "pantry" is supplied for this competition, with items listed in Table 13-2.

Category G: Edible Cold Food

The concept of an edible cold food display demands, in essence, the same criteria as the Mystery Basket concept, and hence can only be executed under a strictly controlled environment. Requirements for the single competitor are as follows:

- *Cooking:* One cold buffet or hors d'oeuvres platter for 8 to 10 portions. The hors d'oeuvres must consist of a minimum of six varieties times the

TABLE 13-2   Communal Pastry Storeroom Supplies

Dairy	Flours, Nuts, Sugars	Miscellaneous Pastry Staples
Milk	All-purpose flour	Apricot jam
Heavy cream	Cake flour	Raspberry jam
Unsalted butter	Pastry flour	Vegetable oil
Sour cream	Cornmeal	Regular shortening
Yogurt	Bread flour	Neutral fruit glaze
Ricotta cheese	High-gluten flour	Instant coffee
Cream cheese	Almond flour	Vanilla extract
Tofu	Hazelnut flour	Lemon extract
Crème fraiche	Almonds (whole, sliced, slivered)	Almond extract
Eggs	Hazelnuts	Powdered gelatin
Margarine	Pecans	Sheet gelatin
Fruits, Produce, Herbs	Walnuts	Baking powder
Minimum: five seasonal fruits	Pine nuts	Baking soda
Oranges	Pistachios	Almond paste
Lemons	Super-fine sugar	Coconut
Limes	Powdered sugar	Long-grain rice
Grapefruits	Brown sugar	Assorted spices: (cinnamon, nutmeg, ginger, allspice, cloves)
Vanilla bean	Granulated sugar	Dry yeast
Fresh mint	Honey	Seeds
Chocolate Products	Corn syrup or glucose	Poppy seeds
Dark chocolate (bittersweet)		Salt
Milk chocolate		Quick oats
White chocolate		Minute tapioca
Cocoa powder		

number of portions. The platter must also present the appropriate salads and garnitures; it should be the same as the cold platter competition with two main items, one salad, and two garnishes.

■ *Pastry:* One buffet platter, 8 to 10 portions of each variety of confectionery or dessert with theme.

Such a show can only be approved if the issuing of quality fresh foods is strictly controlled and proctored. The processing and handling of these foodstuffs must be monitored from beginning to end to verify that it conforms to all sanitation and health guidelines. All finished products must be kept at 45°F. or below without interruption until tasted and evaluated.

The host facility must carry the approval and meet the requirements of the local health department. To successfully execute a competition in this category, the show organizers will need two days, each with an eight-hour shift. The first-day schedule would include menu development; issuing of Mystery Basket; kitchen and station assignment; display time assignment; and seven hours of proctored mise en place, preparation, and cooking time.

The second day is allocated primarily for the competitor to complete the buffet requirements and display at the appropriate time. All the requirements for kitchen setup are the same as in the hot food kitchen, and all procedures must be strictly monitored.

Category H: Ice Carving

This is an exciting category, one where culinarians and artists mingle. Category H, Ice Carving, comprises four subcategories, depending on the number of carvers and the amount of ice to be carved:

■ **Category H/1:** Single block individual freestyle: one person, one block, three hours time limit

■ **Category H/2:** Two-person team, three blocks, three hours

■ **Category H/3:** Three-person team, five blocks, three hours

■ **Category H/4:** Two- or three-person team, 15 to 20 blocks, exhibition carving, 48-hour time limit, outdoors

General guidelines are as follows:

■ Safety is the single most important rule for competitors and spectators. A first safety violation may result in a verbal warning at the discretion of the judges; a second warning will result in disqualification.

■ All competition ice must be carved on the premises, within the specified time limit, and only by the competitor who entered the category. The sole exception is category H/4, exhibition carving, where one helper

167

may be used by each competitor. However, the helper must register with the competitor and sign all waivers. He or she can handle the ice and tools but may not alter the ice in any way. No helpers are allowed for team competitions.

- Display tables for individual freestyle carvings (if provided by the exhibition officials) should have a surface of 48 by 48 inches and have adequate stability and braces.
- A lead judge with a proven background in ice sculpture will supervise the jury. A minimum of three judges with experience in the area of carving will judge, employing an open, or blind, judging system. The decision of the judges is final.
- The lead judge is responsible for conducting the carvers' meeting before the start of the competition. The show's organizing committee should also participate in this meeting and introduce all officials and judges to the competitors.

Guidelines for carving platforms are as follows:

- The platforms should be nonskid, preferably made of wood. Wood pallets are readily available in any convention area. Exterior-grade plywood 1/2 inch by 4 feet by 8 feet will cover two pallets.
- Each carver will need a minimum of two pallets, covered in such a manner and spaced to ensure participants are not too close together. A base of six pallets covered with three sheets of plywood would accommodate a two-or three-person team event; it could be used also for two single carvers working simultaneously. Since most competitions have both single and team events, this should be the standard.
- The surface on which the platforms are placed should be, ideally, cement or nonskid flooring. Plastic sheeting on flooring is dangerous and thus not acceptable.

Venue guidelines are as follows:

- **Power supply:** The power supply must be adequately grounded and be powerful enough to accommodate several 120-volt chain saws operating at the same time (one per competitor). The connections for the power supply should never be standing in water. The engineering staff of the facility should be available at the beginning of the contest to ensure a successful start.
- **Lighting:** Lighting should be bright enough to ensure a safe environment for the competitors, as well as to provide good visibility for judges and spectators.

- **Drainage:** The area where the carvings are composed and displayed should have appropriate drainage so that no standing water is evident.
- **Debris:** The show organizers are responsible for providing one assistant for every four participants on the floor; assistants will clear the area of any debris ice and keep the area clean.
- **Judges' panel:** The judges' panel should have a minimum of three judges, experienced ice sculptors and artist(s), and at least one ACF-approved ice carving judge. It is always advisable to use judges from out of town, particularly for the lead judge position. Media or celebrity judges should be employed for special awards but should not be part of the official scoring. The lead judge should be indicated on the score sheets; he or she should be accomplished in the field of ice carving. If an open system of judging is employed, the members of the jury should be available for a critique with the competitors after the judging. This is an important step in the learning and advancement of ice carving and is consistent with ACF procedures for all food competitions.

Displays are judged in four areas, each worth a possible 10 points:

- Artistic achievement and strength of design
- Craftsmanship: work involved; level of detail and precision; strong lines, symmetrical, of even depth, and uniformity
- Finished appearance: the piece has a finished look and is free of cracks, chips, or excess slush
- Originality and degree of difficulty, uniqueness, original design or composition

Table 13-3 lists safety equipment and authorized carving tools. The responsibilities of an ice carving show's organizers are as follows:

- Issue a liability waiver to each competitor at the time of application; issue the same to each helper, apprentice, or other persons who will be in the working areas. The waiver is intended to relieve ACF and organizers of any responsibility if an accident should occur. This waiver could also include a clause for rights to photograph or film the contest for future advertisement or promotional purposes.
- Secure necessary materials for the setup and construction of the work areas, adequate power supply, drainage, and lighting, as specified above.
- Arrange for personnel to emcee the event; provide an official time clock visible to all competitors; install proper signage for the competitors, to include a scoreboard on which to post the competitors' final scores.
- Provide staff to assist the judges in totaling and averaging scores, and either calculators or computers to ensure accuracy.

TABLE 13-3   Ice Carving Equipment and Tools

Safety Equipment	Authorized Ice Carving Tools*
Protective clothing (no loose scarves, etc.)	Ice tongs; hand saws; five-prong shaver; ice pick
Steel-toed boots	Chain saws (and new spare chains)
Safety glasses	Steam wand
Electrical equipment, grounded	Table with circular saw; level carpenter's dividers
Gloves (cold weather protection)	Drummel; router
Ear plugs	Alcohol/propane burners
Proper lifting equipment (capable of moving ice blocks and finished pieces weighing 300 to 400 pounds)	Draw knife
Adequate drainage	Large compass; string wood ruler
	Extra bars
	Chisels: large flat, long-handle medium flat, long-handle small flat, long-handle large V-shaped, long-handle small V-shaped, long-handle round inside cut and round outside cut

* Power tools only.

Category K: Practical and Contemporary Hot Food Cooking

In this category, individual competitors fabricate and prepare a finished product based on the following main course categories. Competitors must prepare four portions in all K categories, with 60 minutes to fabricate and cook the menu; they have five additional minutes for plating.

- **K-1 Rock Cornish game hen, chicken, or duck:** Fabricate and cook a 1- to 2-pound Rock Cornish game hen or a 2- to 3-pound chicken or a 5- to 6-pound duck, using the whole or part of the bird.
- **K-2 Bone-in pork loin:** Fabricate and cook to specification. Other pork cuts may be included in the dish.
- **K-3 Bone-in veal loin or rack:** Fabricate either choice and cook to specification. Other veal cuts may be included in the dish. Chine bone only may be removed from the rack before the competition.
- **K-4 Bone-in lamb loin or rack:** Fabricate either choice and cook to specification. Other lamb cuts may be included in the dish. Chine bone only may be removed from the rack before the competition.
- **K-5 Game birds:** Choices of game birds can be 1- to 2-pound pheasant,

170

quail(s), squab(s,) partridge(s), or up to 2-pound guinea fowl. Game birds must be fabricated during the competition and cooked as the recipe states.

- **K-6 Bone-in game—venison and antelope, racks, or loin:** Fabricate either choice and cook to specification. Other game cuts may be included in the dish. Chine bone only may be removed from the rack before the competition.
- **K-7 Whole rabbit:** Fabricate and cook to recipe specifications, using the leg and at least one other cut.
- **K-8 Live lobster:** Using 1- to 2-pound lobsters, fabricate and cook to recipe specifications. Other crustaceans/mollusks may be incorporated with this, or other categories, also.
- **K-9 Fish:** Fabricate a 2- to 3-pound flat or round fish. Fish can be eviscerated and scaled, but the head must remain on when brought in. Prepare as recipe specifies.
- **K-10 Customized:** ACF chapters and other organizations wishing to sponsor contemporary hot food competitions that are sponsor-driven or that do not follow the prescribed contemporary format may apply for ACF approval. The standard application must be supplemented with a detailed description of the competition and must be submitted a full six months before the competition. It must have the approval of the Culinary Competition Committee chair. Specialty competitions can also be organized—for example, wild mushrooms, asparagus, seasonal artichoke, a one-hour cook-off with trout, squash, specialty produce, and so on, as long as they are organized to demonstrate the specific skills.

General rules and guidelines, which are applicable to all the above contemporary categories, are as follows:

- Competitors must provide recipes, all ingredients, and a complete diagram or a clear, close-up, color photograph of the signature dish. These should be received by the show chair a minimum of two weeks before the competition. Competitors must also provide copies of their recipes and photographs for the tasting judges.
- No advance preparation or cooking is allowed. Vegetables can be peeled and salads may be cleaned and washed, but not cut or shaped in any form; beans may be presoaked. Exceptions are chopped herbs, shallots, garlic, and mirepoix. Competitors may also bring proteins premarinated, but will be required to demonstrate fabrication of protein and making of marinade.
- Competitors are allowed to bring in only the whole and raw materials in the amounts stated in their recipes. However, the judges may allow vari-

ances in amounts for products that require further preparation (whole fish, meats, etc.). No finished sauces are allowed; however, basic stocks (beef, veal, chicken, vegetable, or fish) may be brought in as necessary for the assignment. No clarified consommés are allowed.

■ Competitors will bring their own tools, including small ware and plain white china (plates, platters, bowls, etc.) on which to display the finished dish.

■ All competitors are required to prescale their recipes. The following ready-made dough may be brought in: puff pastry and phyllo dough.

■ Competitors should use the following guidelines in formulating a balanced, nutritionally sound recipe: Based on overall calories, no more than 30 percent of the daily calories should come from fat; 50 to 60 percent of the daily calories should come from carbohydrates; and 15 to 20 percent of the daily calories should come from proteins.

Category P: Practical and Contemporary Patisserie

This category comprises five subdivisions.

CATEGORY P/1: HOT/WARM DESSERT

Competitors in this subdivision will demonstrate a hot/warm dessert preparation of their choice, according to these guidelines:

■ They have 60 minutes to prepare the dessert, with five additional minutes allocated for serving and judging.

■ Only the raw ingredients and materials, in the amounts stated in the recipe, may be brought in; judges will, however, allow variances in these amounts to account for unforeseen emergencies. No finished sauces are allowed.

■ Competitors must provide a recipe; all ingredients; a diagram of the dessert; and a clear, close-up, color photograph of the signature dish. These must be received a minimum of two weeks before the competition.

■ Competitors will prepare four portions, one for show and critique and three for taste.

■ Ingredients for the recipe can be prescaled and measured; however; no premixing is allowed. The only exception is that cooked ice cream bases and/or sorbet bases may be brought in ready to freeze at the competition site.

■ Competitors must bring their own baking dishes, soufflé, gratin, and so on.

CATEGORY P/2: COMPOSED COLD DESSERT

In this subcategory, individual competitors will demonstrate one composed cold dessert preparation of their choice according to these guidelines:

- Competitors have 90 minutes to prepare the dessert, with five additional minutes for serving and judging. (Note: Additional time is allocated to complete the proper chilling of the dessert, baking of the dessert, and/or make up of any decoration.)
- Competitors may bring in only the raw ingredients and materials in the amount stated in the recipe. Judges will allow variances in these amounts to accommodate unforeseen emergencies. No finished sauces are allowed.
- Competitors must supply, a minimum of two weeks before the competition, a recipe, all ingredients, a diagram of the dessert, and a clear, close-up, color photograph of the signature dish.
- Competitors will prepare four portions, one for show and critique, and three for taste.
- Competitors may bring in an ice cream machine of reasonable size and electrical requirements. Freezers are not permitted; however, the careful and responsible use of dry ice in appropriate containers is permitted.
- Ingredients for the recipe can be prescaled and measured, but no pre-mixing is allowed, except for cooked ice cream bases and/or sorbet bases, which may be brought in ready to freeze at the competition site.

CATEGORY P/3: CAKE DECORATION

Individual competitors in this subcategory will demonstrate cake decoration for a festive occasion, with ornamentation of the competitor's choice. The occasion will either be randomly drawn or be determined in advance by the local committee to coordinate with the theme of the competition. Competitors will follow these guidelines:

- Competitors will have 60 minutes to prepare and decorate the cake, with five additional minutes allocated for serving and judging.
- Competitors will bring in a cake of approximately 10 by 3 inches of any shape (round, oval, square, rectangle, etc.). The cake should be a filled cake, without any final finish. Competitors will finish the cake with glaze, butter cream, whipped cream, chocolate, and so on, and decorate it to fit the occasion specified.
- Decorations cannot be brought in; only the raw materials necessary to make them, for example, marzipan, chocolate, sugar, and so on.
- If batters are used, such as praline, hippen masse, or tuile, these may be brought in batter stage.

- Cakes may be sliced for inspection to ensure that only edible cakes are used; however, cakes will not be tasted.
- All decoration must be edible.
- No tiered cakes are allowed.
- Competitors may bring in an air brush.

CATEGORY P/4: MARZIPAN MODELING

Individual competitors in this subcategory demonstrate skill and craftsmanship in creative marzipan modeling according to these guidelines:

- Competitors have 60 minutes to prepare two different-size figurines. Four of each figure must be prepared for judging, for a total of eight pieces. The use of an air brush is permitted. An additional five minutes will be allocated for presentation and judging.
- Competitors will bring in all necessary raw materials.
- Competitors will bring in decorative platters to display their work.

CATEGORY P/5: DECORATIVE CENTERPIECE

Individual competitors will demonstrate skill and craftsmanship in a creative, decorative centerpiece following these guidelines:

- Competitors have 90 minutes to create a decorative centerpiece of any medium or a composite of media, such as chocolate, sugar, marzipan, pastillage, modeling chocolate, rolled fondant, gum paste, nougat, and so on. An additional five minutes will be allocated for presentation and judging.
- Competitors will be responsible for their own sugar equipment.
- Competitors may bring cooked sugar of their choice; precooked sugars and pistoles are allowed only for the purposes of pulling and blowing.
- Competitors may bring a simple generic base of poured sugar, pastillage, chocolate, nougat, and so on, in simple shapes.
- All decorating of the base must be done on-site.
- Chocolate may be brought in chopped or in pistoles.
- Competitors will supply their own tools for finishing and may supply their own marble slabs.
- Competitors may bring in decorative platters to display their work.
- Competitors may bring in a household-size (small) microwave.
- Competitors must bring in their own measuring scale, warming lamp, and hair dryer (for cooling). Prewarming the sugar and/or chocolate tempering in the staging area is permitted.

Competition organizers need to be cognizant of the following show requirements:

- Decorative centerpieces may require select room temperatures.
- The use of a microwave in this category is imperative, particularly to allow full and elaborate sugar work. From the spectator standpoint, this would greatly enhance the ability to showcase the individual pastry chef's skill and craftsmanship. Electrical requirements must be evaluated before the competition and an adequate power source provided to avoid any problems.

Categories S: Practical—Skill-Based

This, the final, category is actually not a stand-alone entity, as it is designed to be incorporated into the F3 competition format. It may also be used in any of the K categories.

CATEGORY S/1: VEGETABLES
The individual competitors will exhibit knife skills, mise en place, and basic culinary organizational skills. They will have 20 minutes to complete the assignment. No advance preparation is allowed. The competitor is allowed to bring in only the whole and raw materials to execute the assignment. Competitors will bring their own tools, including small ware, cheesecloth and/or towels, and plain glass bowls to display the finished products. They are required to know all basic classical cuts, as they will be called on to demonstrate three different cuts, which will be drawn at random and which could include mandolin skills. Sample of cuts include julienne, brunoise, batonnet, variations of dice, tourné, rondelle, and paysanne. Competitors will use a 1/80 count potato for each cut.

SCORING

As a competitor, you no doubt will be interested in the scoring sheets used by judges in each of the category competitions. Figures 13-1 to 13-9 show them to you.

(FOR CATEGORY E, TEAM BUFFET, ONE SHEET USED PER REQUIREMENT, THEN TOTAL SCORE AVERAGED FOR TEAM MEDAL)

CATEGORY A B C D E G EXHIBIT/COMPETITOR _____

PRESENTATION AND GENERAL IMPRESSION 0-10 _____

GLAZING AND PLATE OR PLATTER DESIGN 0-15 _____

DEGREE OF DIFFICULTY   0-10_____

COMPOSITION AND HARMONY OF INGREDIENTS 0-10 _____

CORRECT PREPARATION AND CRAFTSMANSHIP 0-45 _____

SERVING METHODS AND PORTION 0-10 _____

TOTAL 100 _____

COMMENTS:

JUDGE'S PRINTED NAME:_____

JUDGE'S SIGNATURE: _____

DATE: _____

Figure 13-1
Cold Food Score Sheet

COMPETITOR _____

JUDGE _____

SHOW DATE _____

SUBTOTAL _____

NUMBER OF COURSES _____

SERVICE/TASTING SCORE _____

COMMENTS:

COURSE 1: _____

COURSE 2: _____

COURSE 3: _____

COURSE 4: _____ *(continues)*

JUDGE'S SIGNATURE: _____

Figure 13-2
Category F/G: Hot Food Tasting Score Sheet

Criteria and Points

Serving Methods and Presentation: 15 points

Fresh and colorful, easy-to-eat closely placed items for maintaining temperature; hot/cold serving plate; stylistic but practical)
Modern presentation styles, appetizing food

Portion Size and Nutritional Balance: 10 points

Proper balance of protein, vegetables, and carbohydrates
Weight boundary within the tolerance of total meal. Nutritional breakdown supplied.

Menu and Ingredient Compatibility: 10 points

Do the recipe ingredients complement each other in color, flavor, and texture? Are the ingredients balanced in size and amounts?

Creativity and Practicality: 5 points

Is the dish creative, showing something new or an old idea modernized? Can the dish be prepared for a party of 40 or 100 or be done in an à la carte kitchen?

Flavor, Taste, Texture, and Doneness: 60 points

Do the specified major ingredients carry the dominant flavors?
Do the components fit together? Are the temperatures correct?
Do the textures reflect the cooking technique?
Is the sauce the correct flavor for the meat/fish, and is it the correct consistency and smooth?

INDIVIDUAL COURSE SCORES: 100 points per course based on three courses
Judge's Guideline for Standards
90-100 Points: Gold
79-89 Points: Silver
68-78 Points: Bronze

Figure 13-2
Category F/G: Hot Food Tasting Score Sheet *(Continued)*

COMPETITOR _____

JUDGE _____

SHOW DATE _____

KITCHEN/FLOOR EVALUATION (0-100 POINTS): _____

COMMENTS:

_____
_____
_____
_____

JUDGE'S SIGNATURE:_____

(continues)

Figure 13-3
Category F/G: Kitchen Floor Score Sheet

CRITERIA (MAXIMUM POINTS)

SANITATION/FOOD HANDLING (20) _____
MISE EN PLACE/ORGANIZATION (10) _____
CULINARY AND COOKING TECHNIQUE AND PROPER EXECUTION (45) _____
PROPER UTILIZATION OF INGREDIENTS (15) _____
TIMING/WORKFLOW (10) _____
TOTAL KITCHEN/FLOOR SCORES (100) _____

JUDGE'S GUIDELINE FOR STANDARDS

90-100 Points: Gold
80-89.999 Points: Silver
69-79.999 Points: Bronze

Figure 13-3
Category F/G: Kitchen Floor Score Sheet *(Continued)*

COMPETITOR _____

SHOW DATE _____

	KITCHEN/FLOOR SCORES		SERVICE/TASTING SCORES	
JUDGE 1	0-100 _____	JUDGE 1	0-100 _____
JUDGE 2	0-100 _____	JUDGE 2	0-100 _____
JUDGE 3	0-100 _____	JUDGE 3	0-100 _____
JUDGE 4	0-100 _____	JUDGE 4	0-100 _____
JUDGE 5	0-100 _____	JUDGE 5	0-100 _____

SUBTOTAL _____

DIVIDE BY NUMBER OF JUDGES _____

DIVIDE NUMBER OF COURSES PER COURSE _____

FINAL KITCHEN SCORE _____

TASTING SCORE   COURSE ONE _____   COURSE TWO _____   COURSE THREE _____

FINAL KITCHEN/ FLOOR SCORE _____

FINAL TASTING SCORE OF ALL COURSES + _____

TOTAL = _____

(0-400 POINTS)

FINAL SCORE (SUBTOTAL DIVIDED BY 4) = _____

(0-100 POINTS)

(continues)

Figure 13-4
Category F/G: Hot Food Tally Score Sheet

AWARD/MEDAL _____

VERIFICATION SIGNATURES

SCORES COMPILED BY: _____

SCORES REVIEWED BY: _____

LEAD JUDGE: _____

JUDGE'S GUIDELINE FOR STANDARDS
90-100 Points: Gold
80-89.999 Points: Silver
70-79.999 Points: Bronze

Figure 13-4
Category F/G: Hot Food Tally Score Sheet *(Continued)*

HOST CHAPTER _____

SHOW DATES _____ CATEGORY _____

COMPETITOR NAME

       JUDGE 1 _____

       JUDGE 2 _____

       JUDGE 3 _____

       JUDGE 4 _____

       JUDGE 5 _____

TOTAL POINTS _____   AVERAGE POINTS _____

MEDAL _____

JUDGE VERIFICATION SIGNATURES:

LEAD JUDGE _____

PRINTED NAME _____

Figure 13-5
Judge's Summary Score Sheet

COMPETITOR _____ TEAM_____

SHOW _____ DATE_____

CARVING _____

ARTISTIC ACHIEVEMENT/STRENGTH OF DESIGN (0-10 POINTS) + _____

CRAFTSMANSHIP/WORK INVOLVED (0-50 POINTS) + _____

• DETAIL AND PRECISION _____

• STRONG LINES _____

• PROPORTION _____

• UNIFORM _____

FINISHED APPEARANCE (0-30 POINTS) + _____

• DOES PIECE HAVE A FINISHED LOOK? _____

• FREE OF CRACKS, CHIPS, AND EXCESS SLUSH? _____

ORIGINALITY AND DEGREE OF DIFFICULTY (0-20 POINTS) + _____

• IS CARVING UNIQUE? _____

• GOOD DESIGN OR COMPOSITION? _____

TOTAL SCORE (0-100 POINTS) = _____

COMMENTS:

_____

_____

_____

_____

JUDGE'S SIGNATURE _____

PRINTED NAME _____

Judge's Guideline for Standards
90-100 Points: Gold
80-89.999 Points: Silver
70-79.999 Points Bronze
Form Revised 07/02

Figure 13-6
Ice Carving (Categories H1-4) Score Sheet

HOST CHAPTER _____

SHOW DATES _____ CATEGORY _____

TEAM/COMPETITOR

FINAL SCORE   AWARD

LEAD JUDGE _____ PRINTED NAME: _____

JUDGE _____

JUDGE _____

JUDGE _____

Figure 13-7
Competition
Summary Score
Sheet

COMPETITOR _____ TEAM_____

SHOW _____ DATE_____

MENU/ITEM: _____

ORGANIZATION (5 POINTS)

SANITATION/WORK HABITS (0-5) _____

UTILIZATION OF INGREDIENTS AND USE OF ALLOTTED TIME (0-5) _____

COMMENTS:

COOKING SKILLS AND CULINARY TECHNIQUES (25 POINTS)

CREATIVITY, SKILLS, CRAFTSMANSHIP (0-5) _____

SERVING/PORTION SIZE (0-5) _____

COMMENTS:

_____

_____

_____

_____

TASTE (40 POINTS)

FLAVOR, TEXTURE (0-10) _____

INGREDIENT COMPATIBILITY AND NUTRITIONAL BALANCE (0-5) _____

PRESENTATION (0-5) _____

TOTAL SCORE (0-100 POINTS) = _____

COMMENTS:

JUDGE'S SIGNATURE _____

PRINTED NAME _____

Figure 13-8
Categories K
and P/1-2: Hot
Food Cooking
and Patisserie

COMPETITOR _____ TEAM_____

SHOW _____ DATE_____

MENU/ITEM: _____

ORGANIZATION (5 POINTS)

SANITATION/WORK HABITS (0-05) _____

UTILIZATION OF ALLOTTED TIME (0-05) _____

COMMENTS:

PRESENTATION (05 POINTS)

OVERALL IMPACT OF DISPLAY (0-10) _____

ORIGINALITY (0-5) _____

COMMENTS:

WORKMANSHIP (30 POINTS)

USE OF VARIOUS TECHNIQUES (0-15) _____

UNIFORMITY (0-5) _____

EXACTNESS OF SKILLS DISPLAYED (0-10) _____

KNOWLEDGE OF SKILLS DISPLAYED (0-10) _____

TOTAL SCORE (0-100 POINTS) = _____

COMMENTS:

JUDGE'S SIGNATURE _____

PRINTED NAME _____

Figure 13-9
Categories P/3-5: Practical and Contemporary Patisserie, Skill-Based

International Culinary Competitions

To American chefs and cooks, the international culinary competition arena is an exciting, and sometimes overwhelming, experience—though I have often wondered why, given that many of these events, like ours, are just local exhibits and contests for those who live near the venues. But there's no denying the thrill of a trip overseas, to compete among chefs from other countries, who cook with such passion—reckless abandon even. From my point of view, the purpose of the international culinary competition is to serve as the display window to our profession, to enable the world to see—and, of course, taste—the progress being made in the field of cookery.

I'll never forget my first experience in international competition: it was in 1983, at the Hotel Olympia in London, when I was working for TrustHouse Forte a leading hotel, restaurant, and catering company with branches in the United Kingdom and United States. The Hotel Olympia is a renowned culinary competition that is held every two years where chefs, cooks, bakers, pastry chefs, and culinarians compete daily over four days in a variety of competitions, from cold food displays, pastry, and centerpiece work that includes marzipan, sugar, chocolate, and salt dough. This competition venue is also famous for its hot food competitions that run daily and at a very fast pace, with a large number of participants in each contest. In fact, the ACF contemporary competitions are a spinoff from those at Hotel Olympia, which led us to recognize the need to bring this aspect of cookery to the States.

Another memorable international experience was my first trip to Frankfurt, Germany, for the IKA, in 1984, when I was apprentice to Fritz Sonnenschmidt, Certified Master Chef (CMC), when he was on the International Chefs city team from New York. Chef Sonnenschmidt was then the culinary dean at the Culinary Institute of America, in Hyde Park, New York, and a seasoned competitor. He had won many awards and had participated as a member of the 1976 ACF national culinary team. I have been at every "Olympics" since then, first as a team chef for a city team and then as the manager/captain for the ACF national culinary team (in 2000 and 2004). And I look forward to serving as the manager in 2008, which will be my last hurrah.

The IKA, for many chefs, is Mecca, where cooking brings unity; where everyone speaks the same language, the language of food; where national politics are of no concern; and where chefs show the world how they can make a difference through the culinary arts. I wish I could adequately describe to you the adrenaline rush and the emotional ups and downs I experienced at these international events—which, for me, were as intense, if not more so, in 2004 than in 1984. For everyone who comes to IKA—the chefs, the cooks, the spectators, the judges, and fans—it is a genuine celebration and show of commitment to this great profession and craft.

After participating in these competitions and many more in other parts of the world, I have come to this conclusion: The purpose of the international arena is to define the trends—what is new for today's cooks and customers. As such, the displays and cookery demonstrated at international shows serve as the display window to our profession, where the novice cook, apprentice, and the public can see, taste, and watch the progress being made in the field of cookery.

But I'd be remiss if I did not mention something else I discovered at these international competitions—something I find troubling: Other countries respect the art of cookery in the competition setting more than we do in the United States. There, even the top chefs at the best restaurants participate in these events, whether by cooking, giving demonstrations, or judging; and they are encouraged by their restaurant and hotel associations to host culinary exhibits and competitions. They work closely with the host country chefs' association to produce shows that generate great interest among professionals and the public alike. Chefs in many countries receive government assistance, or help from their tourism boards or other financial backing, to pursue their quest to represent their countries and compete in high-profile competitions. In short, around the globe, cooking competitions are a very important aspect of the culture, embraced even by the press. We in this country, in contrast, have a very difficult time getting the time of day from our press—even industry trade publications fail to pay adequate attention to our overseas accomplishments. Case in point: The 2004 ACF Team USA won its first gold medal since 1988 in the hot kitchen, the world championship in the hot food category, third overall in a field of 32 countries, yet we received no coverage.

Initially, the ACF developed its culinary competition program to give chefs in this country competition venues in which they could demonstrate to the public their accomplishments. Efforts are currently underway to expand our reach, by developing a far-reaching public relations program to promote our profession to the general public, to educate them about what we do as culinarians.

Part of the reason for the different attitude toward the culinary arts in this country versus overseas is, simply, an entirely different way of thinking about food in general, from the homemaker who prepares daily meals for her family to the most prestigious chefs cooking the latest and greatest cuisines for a diverse clientele. This was brought home to me one year in Luxembourg, while I was there to compete in the Culinary World Cup. Shopping with my teammates at a great market, we were dazzled by the remarkable displays of food—the sheer variety was mind-boggling. Shopping among us, I noticed, were homemakers and others in the general public who were picking and choosing the best quality of food for their homes, just as the chefs were doing for their restaurants. My point is, there, food is a priority in life, not just an entertainment trend. So it is not surprising that chefs overseas receive support for their competition training; it is seen as a valuable addition to their professional education, as well as a way to meet and cook with other colleagues.

NAMING NAMES IN THE INTERNATIONAL ARENA

There are many international culinary competitions, too many to list here. I will, however, name a few that are special: First, the aforementioned IKA, or Culinary Olympics (www.culinary-olympics.com), as it is called, which is held every four years; the World Cup in Luxembourg, likewise, held every four years; the Culinary Master's in Basel, Switzerland, held every six years, and is by invitation only; the Singapore Cup, a grand show, held every two years; and Scothot, in Glasglow, Scotland (http://site.org.uk/scothot/), which rotates a senior class and a junior class every two years For more on these events, go to the Web sites of the event organizers.

SETTING THE STANDARD

Needless to say, in the international arena, standards are very high—you better be "on your game" when you step into a kitchen to cook or display a cold program. Whether you participate as an individual competitor, student, or as a member of a team, competing in the international arena is an experience not to be missed, leaving one with the satisfaction of accomplishment.

The international standards vary, depending on the level you cook at. For example, a gold medal won by an individual at IKA is different from a gold medal won by a regional team, different again from a gold won by a national team—that is, all golds are not created equal.

The reason is expectations. When a national team enters the kitchen or submits their display, a minimum standard is expected, and that is what they are judged against. The expectation is that they know how to cook and work in a kitchen, thus they are expected to perform at a very high level; if they do not, points are deducted. There is no leniency, for chefs at that level are not expected to make mistakes..

It is precisely these high expectations that drive many chefs to test themselves in this way—it is their proving ground, if you will. In the process they push themselves to practice, to work with other top chefs, to get "beat up" and head back to the drawing board time after time. They know it is the only way to get better at what they do, to be better than they ever thought possible.

HAVING A GAME PLAN

When I began to compete, I entered the smaller shows, with fewer competitors, but I learned quickly that to be one of the best, you need to compete with the best. But to compete on the international scale, you need a game plan—similar to the action plans I described earlier. I recommend you devise a three- to five-year plan, especially if one of your goals is to try out for Culinary Team USA. By gaining competition experience at this level, you improve your chances of making the team—and for succeeding over your lifetime in this profession.

Here are some helpful hints and suggestions to guide you as you begin to make your three- to five-year plan for your international journey:

- Commit to the experience as a long-term goal. Many chefs who participate in global competitions do so for 8, 12, and 20-plus years. To excel and establish a reputation in this type of venue takes a major commitment of time and energy.

- Attend one of the international competitions first as an observer, to see for yourself what happens at an international show—the quality of presentations, the type of displays, the pace, and so on.
- Recognize up front the challenges—with language, travel arrangements, products, and so on.
- Organize, organize, organize. Plan, plan, plan. Use the many tools and strategies described in this book to assist you.
- Enter as many ACF-approved or local shows that you can in the United States, to gain show experience, to raise your skill level, and to get your competitive juices flowing.
- Study all you can in regard to techniques, styles of food, and the development of flavors. Learn how to demonstrate very solid fundamental skills. Craftsmanship is highly regarded and expected in both the hot and cold kitchen.
- In an international competition, stick to your cuisine. It is expected that chefs will focus on the cuisine of their countries. Yes, America is a melting pot, but it is also the foundation of many great dishes and regional cuisines that are unquestionably American.
- Strive to be creative, but be sensible, to ensure that your concept and food can be understood easily by those from other countries.
- Seek out chefs who have "been there and done that"—successfully—and can give you advice, and perhaps critique your display or hot food. Find out from them the challenges they faced, what they feel worked and what did not.
- Do not get discouraged. If you meet with defeat initially, stick with it; be determined—remember your commitment to a long-range plan. It is a shame that in this country we do not often see students follow a natural progression, from the youth team to the regional level then to the national team. That is why many countries have an advantage over our teams today: in this country, too many who have some experience walk away far too early. The ACF USA culinary teams of the early 1980s were together for three IKA competitions, with some members involved and competing since 1972. That is commitment and perseverance.

 ## CONCLUSION

In closing, I want to say that when it comes to competing, in particular on the international front, so much depends on your approach. Don't think, "If

I get the opportunity ..."; *make* the opportunity to see an international competition, to attend a trade show where you can experience the host country's cuisine. These are the kinds of educational ventures that will inspire you and keep you coming back for more. But whether it is international, local, or regional, *get involved*, cook to learn, show your food, and do it with pride. I promise you, the rewards will be incalculable, in the forms of friendship, networking, education, and life experience.

Epilogue

Motivational quotations have always inspired me. They express deep meaning in very few words; they can set a tone or direction for success. When ACF Culinary Team USA came to the Westchester Country Club team headquarters for our practice sessions, a sign read: "You do not win silver, you lose gold."

In my kitchens, too, I hang signs—the biggest and most common one being, "Culinary Pride," which to me signifies a culture, an environment, where everyone is on the same page. This is essential to success in the competition arena and in the workaday kitchen. It gives purpose, reminding us every day why we do what we do. Reading something that causes the light-bulb in the head to go on, to stir the passion, and fuel the desire is a good thing. Words of wisdom will never fail to push you to be the best you can be, to cook the best you can cook, which, after all, is why chefs, cooks and culinarians get up every day.

For the ACF culinary team 2000, the motivational quote we kept in our toolbox was, "Defeat is worse than death because you have to live with defeat." Yes, it was extreme, but we were representing the ACF members, the cuisine of America, and all our country's cooks, chefs, and culinarians, and we did not want to fail them, or ourselves.

We did not forget, however, that the most important thing was not the outcome, but that, at the end of the day we did our best, we gave 100 percent of our talent and ability, while learning along the way to become better cooks.

So I remind you, too, that no matter how good a chef you are, there will be another one better. And, again, that is what is so great about ACF competitions: you are first measured by the standard set forth; you can earn a gold medal if your work is up to the standard. Yes, winning is a great feeling of accomplishment. I will never forget standing on that podium in Erfurt, Germany, seeing every person there rise from their chairs as our national anthem played because we had won the hot food championship. But I also remember the first competition with the team in 1999, when we took all silver at the culinary classic. Though I was proud of what we accomplished in only a seven weeks preparation time, I determined to do better, to place a priority on perfecting the process of team competition on an international level. So in 2003 we swept the classic; we were the first United States team to ever win the event since its inception. My point again: Learn, perfect your skills, be committed, because the road is long and will have some bumps and detours. With diligence and the will to learn, to push yourself, and raise the bar, you will be successful.

NOTE
Unless otherwise cited, all quotes are from the author.

Here, then, I offer you a selection of some of my favorite motivational quotations, which I encourage you to reproduce and post wherever they can be seen every day.

Winning is not a sometime thing, it is an all-the-time thing.
—Vince Lombardi

You don't cook food right once in a while, you need to cook food right all the time.

Winning and a commitment to excellence is a habit.
—Vince Lombardi

Every time you step into the kitchen be committed to being the best you can be.

It is good to be smart and talented, but remember to cook from your heart.

Give every fiber of your being to achieving your goals and objectives.
—Words to live by

Excellence can be yours if you see the invisible, feel the intangible, strive for the impossible.

Meet challenges with an eager attitude and a curious mind.

Set your expectations a notch higher than others, then strive to exceed your expectations.

Regard adversity as a building block, not a stumbling block.

Offer respect as readily as you expect it.

Listen to your inner voice, not the voices of skeptics.

Know that real danger in life is doing nothing.

Use the intensity of your disappointments to fuel your endeavors.

Live by the decisions you make and move on without regret.

Rise every time you fall. Use your imagination to explore the possibilities.

One moment in time to be the best we can be.

*The roots of true achievement lie in the will to become
the best that you can become.*
—Harold Taylor

Practice.

*A good chef must be serious about cooking;
when a chef prepares food, he or she must respect it.*

Dedication, Endurance, and Achievement

*We will use classical techniques to paint an
impressionistic American culinary canvas.*

*We must always remember that world competition is never won
by one or two individuals, but through the total uncompromising and
personal dedication and unflattering effort on behalf of the entire team.*
—Chef Ferdinand Metz, CMC, 1983

Glossary

Acidulated water   Cold water with vinegar or a citrus juice, used to keep items such as apples from tuning brown while preparing.

Adjust   To taste and regulate the seasonings before serving, to achieve the intended flavor.

Aiguillette   A thin strip of meat, poultry, or fish.

al dente   Italian for "to the bite"; used primarily to describe pasta that is cooked only until it gives a slight resistance when one bites into it; ideally the food is neither soft nor underdone.

Allumette   Matchstick size and shape.

Appetizer   (also: hors d'oeuvre or amuse bûche) A small offering of food or beverage served before or as the first course of a meal.

Aroma   Fragrance; the smell of the food.

Aspic   A jelly produced from the stock of meat, fish, or fowl, or a liquid held together with natural gelatin by-products and clarified. Clear meat, poultry, or fish jelly can be made or purchased.

Bain-marie   A steam table or double-boiler insert that keeps food warm; at times, used to cook with, such as Sauce Hollandaise.

Bake   To cook in an oven, surrounding the food with dry heat of a specific temperature. A convection oven will circulate the dry heat and cook at a more even and rapid rate.

Bard   To wrap meat with bacon or salt pork.

Baste   To pour drippings, fat, or stock over food while cooking.

Béchamel   a French mother sauce made by thickening milk with a white roux and adding seasonings; also called cream or white sauce.

Bite size   A portion that easily fits into the mouth, such as an appetizer.

Blanch To immerse food briefly into boiling water, then plunge into cold water. Blanching will firm the flesh while heightening the color and flavor. It is also used to loosen skins for removal from such items as tomatoes and pearl onions.

Boil To cook in a liquid that has reached a temperature of 212°F and where bubbles are rising rapidly and breaking the surface.

Bouquet Aroma; a term used to describe the fragrance of wines and other foods.

Bouquet garni A combination of herbs tied in cheesecloth, which are used to flavor stocks and stews and are removed before serving.

Braise To cook meat by searing in fat, then simmering in a covered pot with one-third of flavorful stock or broth.

Brine A solution of salt and water used in pickling and cleansing. Brine draws natural sugars and moisture from foods and forms lactic acids, which protect the food against spoilage.

Broil To cook food by placing it a measured distance below direct, dry heat.

Bruise To partially crush an ingredient, such as herbs or peppercorns, to release its flavor and make it more potent.

Brunoise Finely diced vegetables.

Chaud French for "hot."

Deglaze To add liquid such as wine, stock, or water to the bottom of a pan to dissolve and lift the caramelized drippings and flavors from the pan.

Dredge To coat with dry ingredients such as flour or bread crumbs.

Dust To sprinkle with sugar, spices, powders, or flour.

Emince To cut fine, or slice thin.

Espagnole A mother brown sauce.

Farce Forcemeat or stuffing.

Farci Stuffed

Forcemeat Ground meat or meats, mixed with seasonings and used for flavor, moisture, and texture.

Froid French for "cold."

Galantine A cold jellied dish of boned chicken, veal, game, or fish

Garde manager The person in charge of the cold, pantry, or garde department.

Gastrique A French term meaning to form a glaze by reduction.

Garnish To decorate; to use food for garniture.

Garniture: French for "garnish."

Gelatin A colorless, odorless, and flavorless mixture of proteins made from animal bones, connective tissues, and other parts, along with certain algae (agar). When dissolved in a hot liquid and then cooled, gelatin forms a jellylike substance used as a thickener and stabilizer in molded desserts, cold soups, chaud froid creations, and the like, and as a fining agent in beer and wine.

Glaze Shiny coating applied to a food, such as aspic or apricot glaze. Glaze can be also created by the cooking process, such as basting during meat cookery or adding an egg wash to bread or pastry items.

Herb bouquet A mixture of herbs tied together and used for seasoning in soups, sauces, and stocks.

Hors d'oeuvre   Petite appetizers or relishes, served at a reception before the meal. In Europe, can be the first plate.

Ice bath   A mixture of ice and water used to chill a food or beverage rapidly.

Infuse   To steep herbs and other flavorings such as vanilla beans, cinnamon sticks, etc., in boiling liquid.

Infusion   Liquid derived from steeping herbs, spices, etc.

Julienne   A cut of meat, poultry, or vegetables that is 1/8 by 1/8 by 1-1/2 inches long.

Jus   Usually refers to the natural juice from meat or a product after cooking.

Larding   Salt pork strips inserted into meat with a special needle. Used to add flavor and moisture to meat.

Lardon   Julienne of bacon. Strips of salt pork used for larding

Liaison   A binding agent made up of egg yolks and cream, used for thickening soups and sauces.

Marinate   To cover food with a dry or liquid marinade that is seasoned and then infused for a specified amount of time before cooking to make it more flavorful, moist, and/or tender.

Measuring cups   1. Vessels, usually made of plastic or metal, with a handle and a rim that is level with the top measurement specified; used to measure the volume of dry substances and generally available in a set of 1/4-, 1/3-, 1/2-, and 1-cup capacities; metric measures are also available. 2. Vessels, usually made of glass, plastic, or metal, with a handle and a spout that is above the top line of measurement; specifically used to measure the volume of a liquid and generally available in 1-, 2-, and 4 cup to 1gallon capacities; metric measures are also available. Also known as glass cup measures.

Mince   To grind or chop fine.

Mise en place   French for everything in its place. In the context of cooking, refers to having all the ingredients necessary for a dish prepared and ready to combine up to the point of cooking.

Mold   To shape food, usually by pouring the liquefied food, chocolate, or mousse into a form. When the item is cold, it retains the shape of the form.

Pan broil   To cook in an uncovered skillet from which the fat is poured off during cooking.

Pan fry   To cook in an uncovered skillet in small amount of shortening.

Parboil   To cook partially by boiling for a short period of time.

Planking   A style of baking or broiling meat or fish on a piece of hard wood that has flavor characteristics.

Poach   To cook in liquid held below the boiling point.

Pound (in cooking)   To flatten food, such as veal cutlets, with a heavy tool. The process is also used to tenderize tough pieces of fish and meat.

Purée   To process a food into a smooth paste, usually with a blender or food processor, or by pressing the food through a fine sieve or food mill.

Quenelle   A poached dumpling (oval shaped), usually made of veal or chicken.

Render   To melt fat away from surrounding meat.

Roulade   A food rolled around a stuffing.

Sachet bag   Cloth bag filled with select herbs; used to season soups or stocks.

Sear   To brown the surface of a meat quickly by cooking in a little fat at a very high heat in order to seal in the meat's juices and create a rich color before finishing by another method.

Season   To enhance a food's flavor by adding salt, pepper, herbs, and other spices.

Shred   To cut into long narrow strips, usually with a grater or sharp knife. Today, shredding is often accomplished with the aid of a food processor.

Shredded   Food that has been processed into long, slender pieces; similar to julienne.

Sieve   To strain liquid from food through the fine mesh or perforated holes of a strainer or sieve.

Simmer   To cook liquid at a temperature just below the boiling point, low enough that tiny bubbles just begin to break beneath the surface around the edge of the pan.

Stock   A rich extract of soluble parts of meat, fish, poultry, etc. A basis for soups or gravies.

Sweat   A method of cooking vegetables in simmering butter. Also called "fat steaming."

Toss   To mix with a rising and falling action.

Truss   To bind poultry for roasting with string or skewers

Velouté   A sauce made with veal stock, cream, and tightened with a white roux.

Water bath   The French call this cooking technique *bain-marie*. It consists of placing a container (baking pan, bowl, soufflé dish, etc.) of food in a large, shallow pan of warm water, which surrounds the food with gentle heat. The food may be cooked in this manner either in an oven or on top of a range. This technique is designed to cook delicate dishes such as custards, sauces, and mousses without breaking or curdling them. It can also be used to keep cooked foods warm.

Zest   The thin, brightly colored, outermost skin layer of citrus fruit (the rind), which contains flavorful aromatic oils and is removed with the aid of a zester, paring knife, or vegetable peeler.

Index